Drawn Together

Uplifting Comics on the

Curious Journey Through Life and Love

Leah Pearlman

A TarcherPerigee Book

tarcherperigee

An imprint of Penguin Random House LLC
375 Hudson Street
New York, New York 10014

Most TarcherPerigee books are available at special quantity discounts for bulk purchase for sales
promotions, premiums, fund-raising, and educational needs. Special books or book excerpts also can
be created to fit specific needs. For details, write: SpecialMarkets@penguinrandomhouse.com.

LIBRARY OF CONGRESS CATALOGING-IN-PUBLICATION DATA
Names: Pearlman, Leah, artist.
Title: Drawn together : Uplifting comics on the curious journey
through life and love / Leah Pearlman.
Description: New York, New York : TarcherPerigee, 2016.
Identifiers: LCCN 2016007416 | ISBN 9780143110248 (hardback)
Subjects: LCSH: Comics, strips, etc. | BISAC: SELF-HELP / Personal Growth /
Happiness. | HUMOR / Form / Comic Strips & Cartoons. | SELF-HELP /
Personal Growth / General.
Classification: LCC NC1429.P388 A4 2016 | DDC 741.5/6—dc23

Printed in the United States of America
1   3   5   7   9   10   8   6   4   2

♥

To my mom, Sue, Joanna and Scott.
Your unceasing, unflinching, unimaginable love and support
make this book (and everything else) possible.
Thank you.

And to Dad, for having everything to do with who I am.
I love you and miss you.

Contents

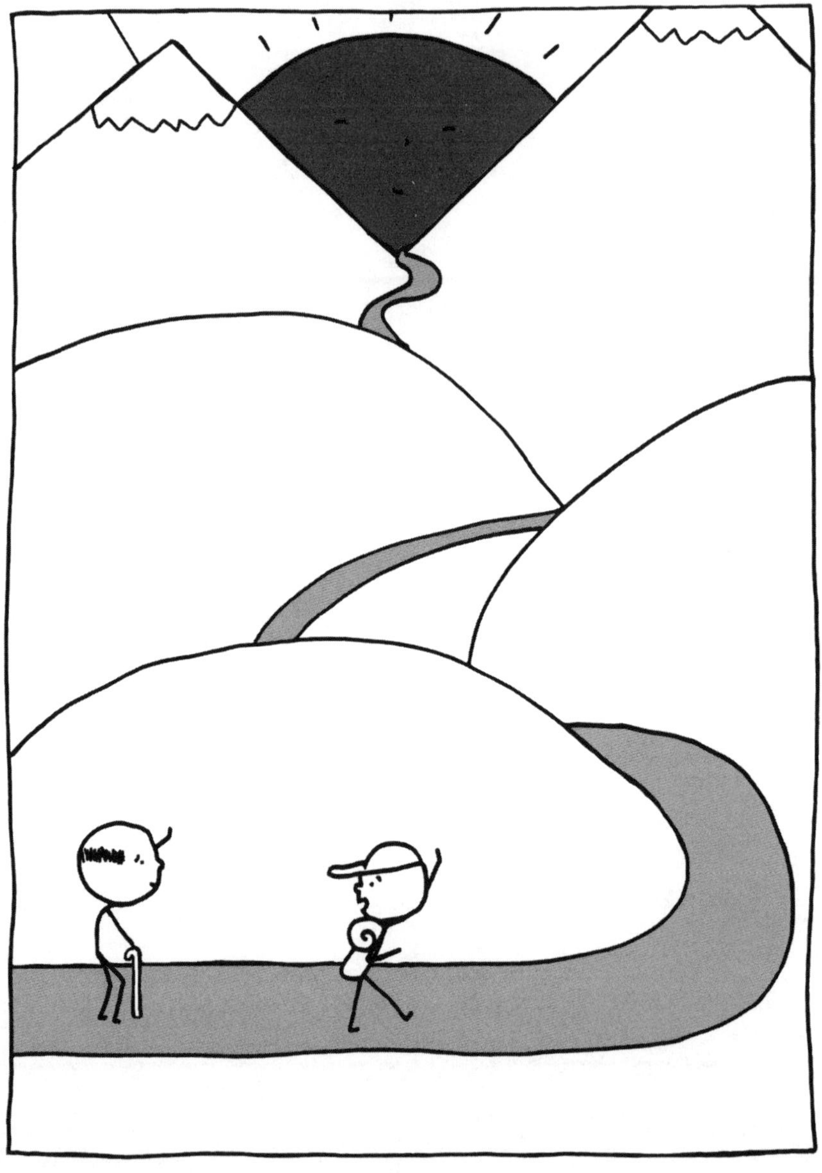

"You have the worst of it behind you now."

"But I have only just begun."

"That's what I mean...

You have begun."

—John O'Donohue, *To Bless the Space Between Us*

Introduction

Hi, I'm Leah. I wrote this book for you. No, really, I did! You may think that's strange because we've probably never met, so let me explain.

Several years ago I had an awesome job at Facebook, fantastic friends, and a huge house with a hot tub...but something wasn't right. My life seemed perfect from the outside, so I couldn't understand what was wrong.

Perhaps I should mention that around this time my dad was diagnosed with lung cancer. Other than asking how he was, from time to time, I mostly tried to ignore it. I was sure he'd be okay...wouldn't he?

Still, when the doctor called to say the cancer was in remission I felt immensely relieved. So much so, that I drew a simple stick-figure comic strip about my family getting the good news, and I posted it on Facebook (obviously).

I don't know what compelled me to use that particular format, but revealing myself through a comic felt good, really good. It allowed me to find the light within something dark.

The next week, I posted another comic, and then another. I began drawing whatever was happening in my life: the ups and downs, getting lost, getting found, the breakthroughs and breakups. Three years later, when my dad's cancer returned, I drew my way through fury. After he passed away, I drew my way through grief.

It seemed that the more I drew what was honest and true, the more others were saying, "Me too!" I called my drawings Dharma Comics; dharma is a Buddhist term for "truth." I watched as hundreds and then thousands of people recognized themselves in these little stick figures and began sharing them with others. We were all connecting around our common human experience.

As I mentioned, before this all happened my life looked great on the outside. But what was going on inside? Dharma Comics gave me the courage to finally look.

And do you know what I found? Me! A perfectly human human. Made up of goodness and fear, beauty and pain, yearning and humor, sweetness and shame—and most of all, love. In the end, the only thing that had been missing was my ability to welcome it all.

Drawn Together is a collection of the most beloved Dharma Comics from the last seven years, as well as many that have never been seen. It's organized into sections that explore human themes that draw us all together: learning to love ourselves and each other, surviving hard times, choosing a right path, and finding stillness amidst the noise. (There's even a surprise at the end, a few little somethings to share with your friends.)

So as I said, this book is for you. It's an invitation from my perfectly imperfect person to yours to go ahead and look inside, and to welcome whatever you find. Because whatever you're going through, whatever you feel, someone else has been there, someone understands. We are never, ever alone.

With love,

Leah

Drawn Together

One:

Loving Me

Learning How to Love

Can you love your crazy?
Can you love your sane?
Can you trust your foolish heart?
Embrace your scattered brain?

Can you love your tears?
Can you love your worry?
Can you hear your darkest fears?
And listen to your fury?

Can you love your inner child?
Your body as you age?
Can you love your wild side
Release it from its cage?

If you're thinking "NO!"
To some of the above,
Then can you love the part of you
That's learning how to love?

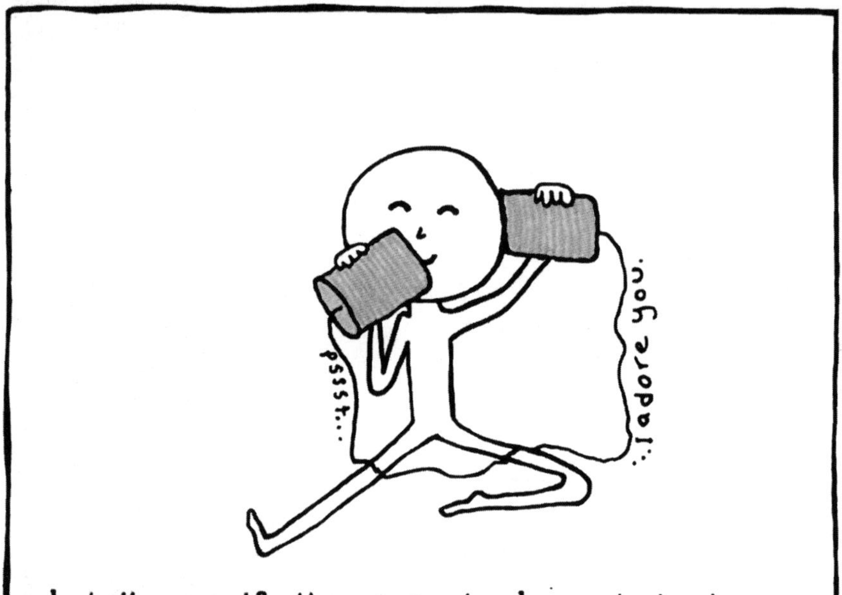
psssst...
...I adore you.

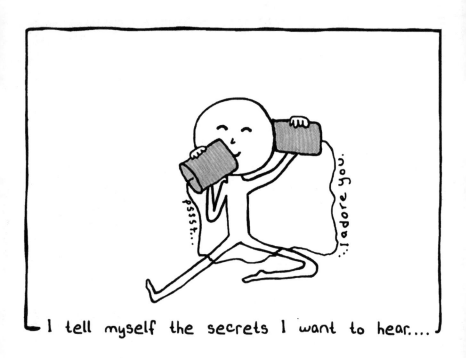

I tell myself the secrets I want to hear....

I never stop surprising myself.

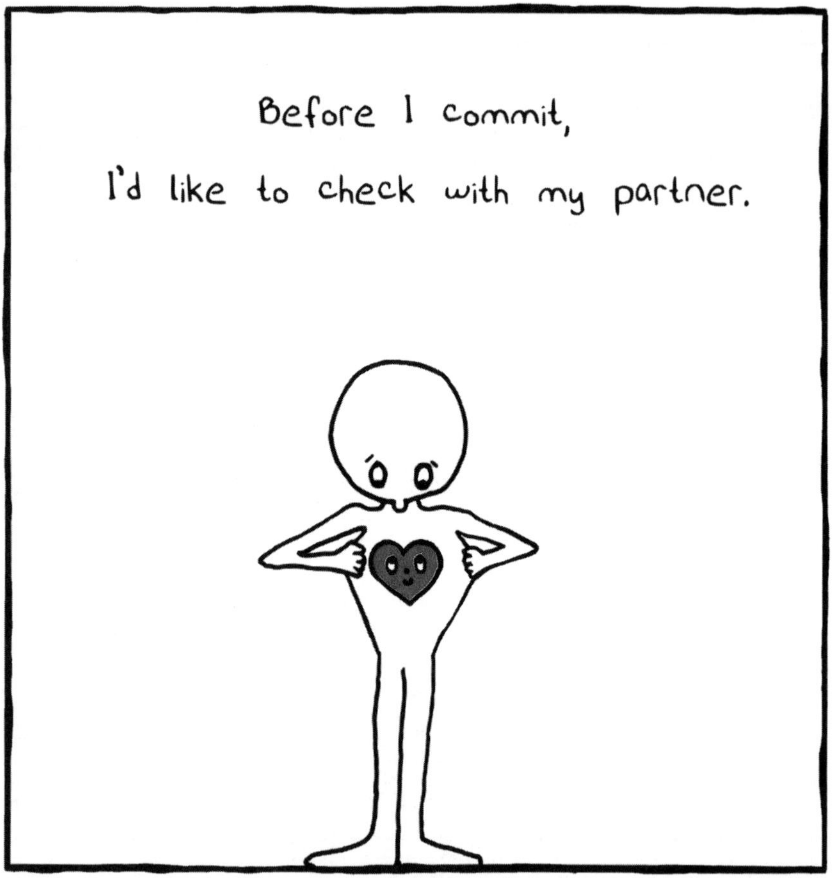
Before I commit,
I'd like to check with my partner.

Something worth protecting.

"Go only as fast as your

s l o w e s t

part...

...feels safe to go."

—Robyn L. Posin

When the burden feels heavy,
it helps to remember...
We're not here.

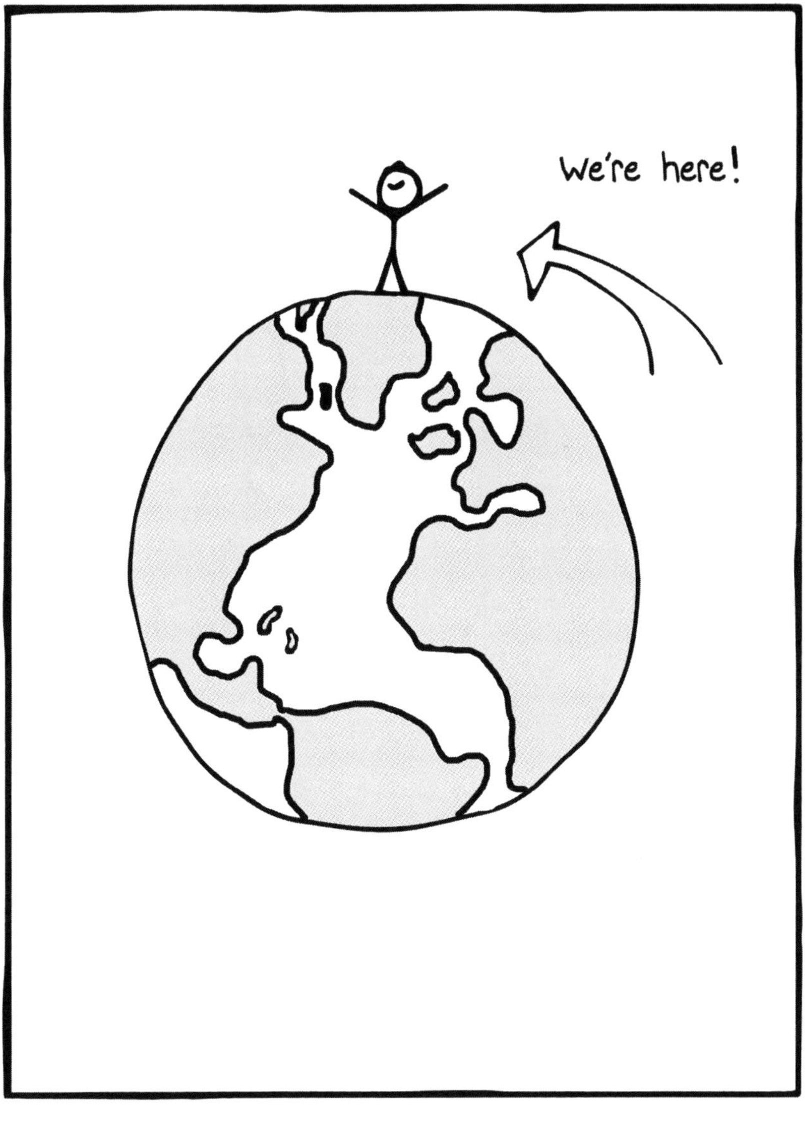
We're here!

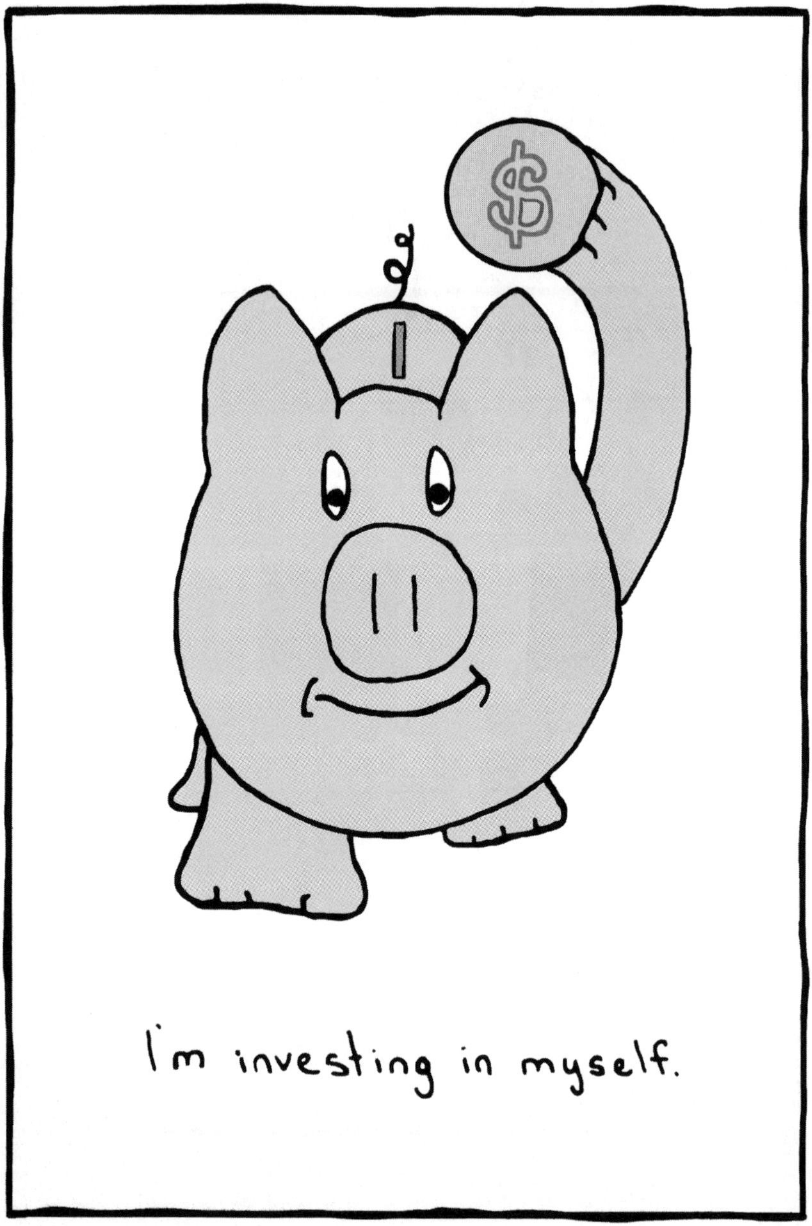
I'm investing in myself.

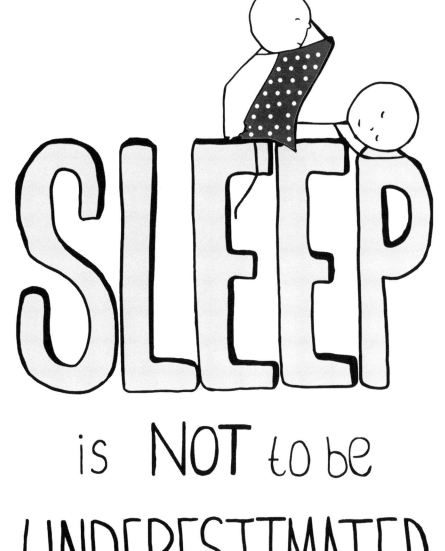

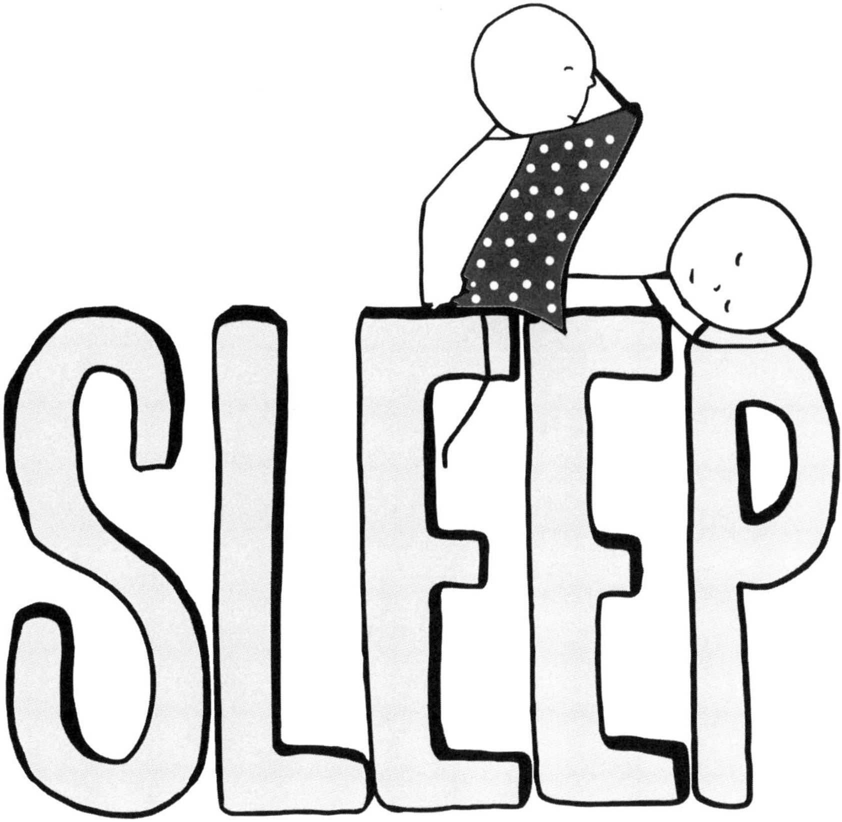
SLEEP

is NOT to be UNDERESTIMATED

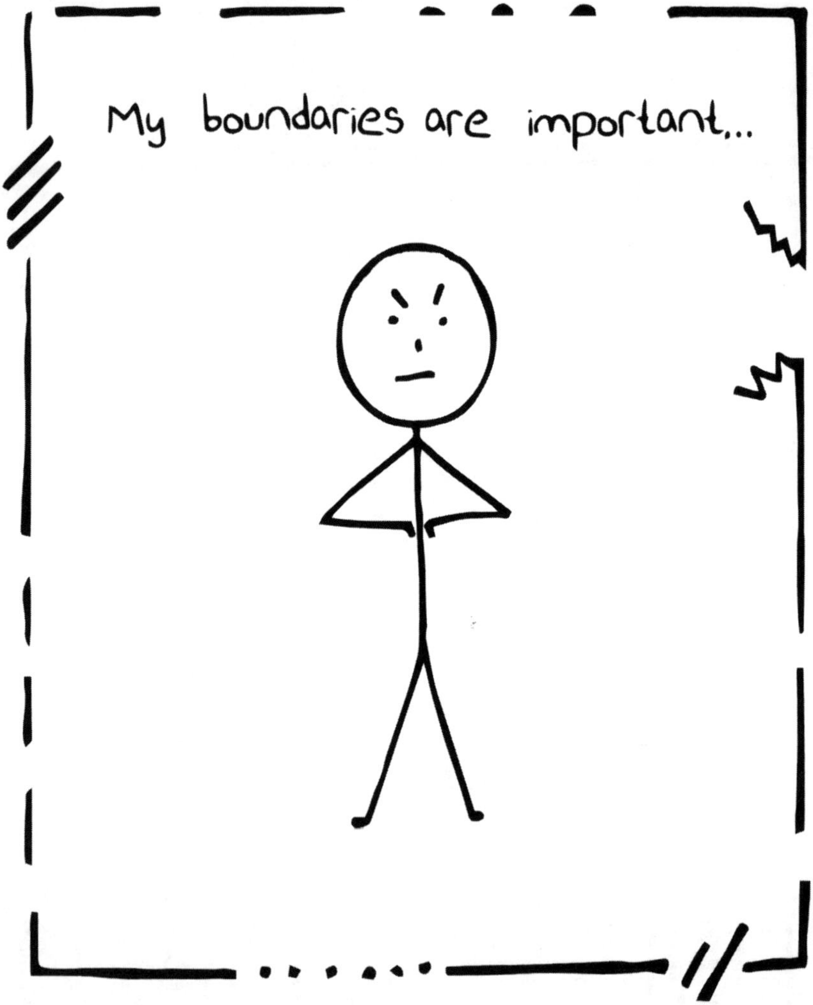
My boundaries are important...

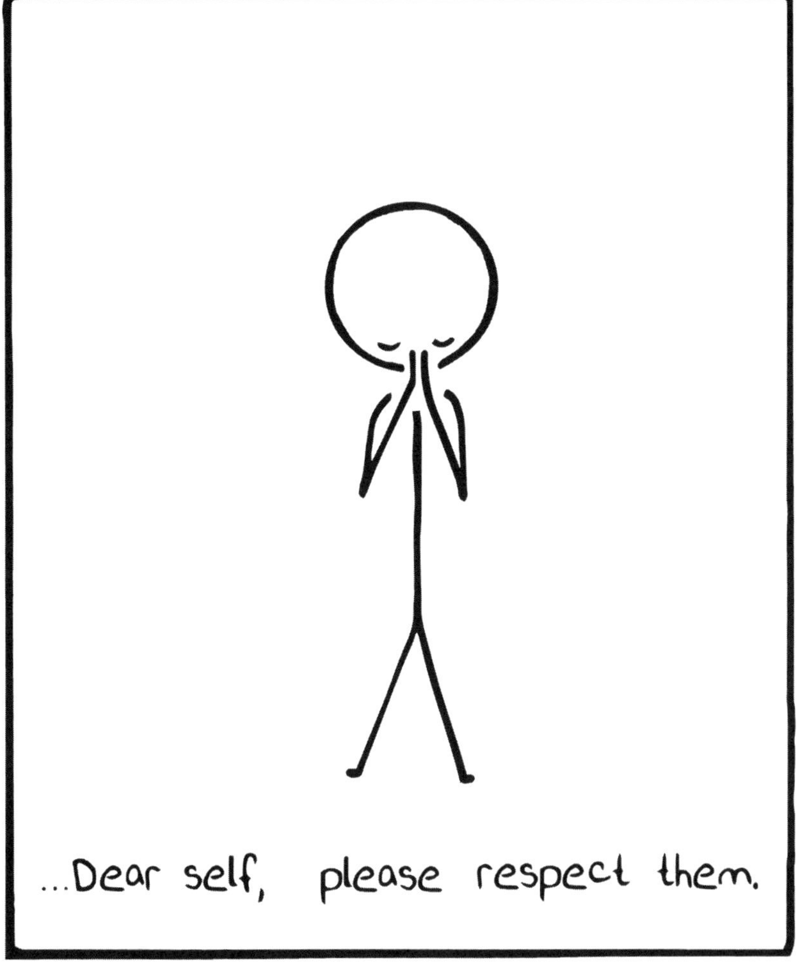
...Dear self, please respect them.

I'm not saying no...

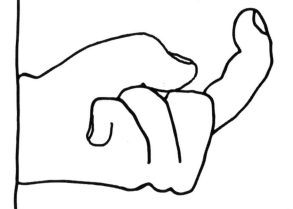

I'm saying YES! to something else.

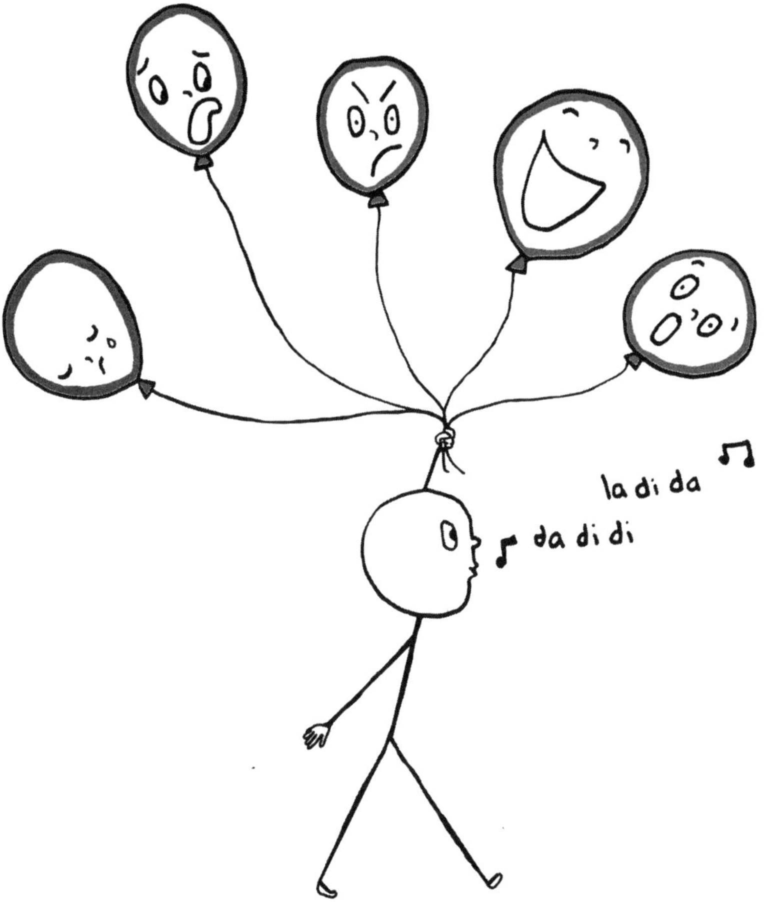
la di da
da di di

I'm learning to hold my emotions lightly.

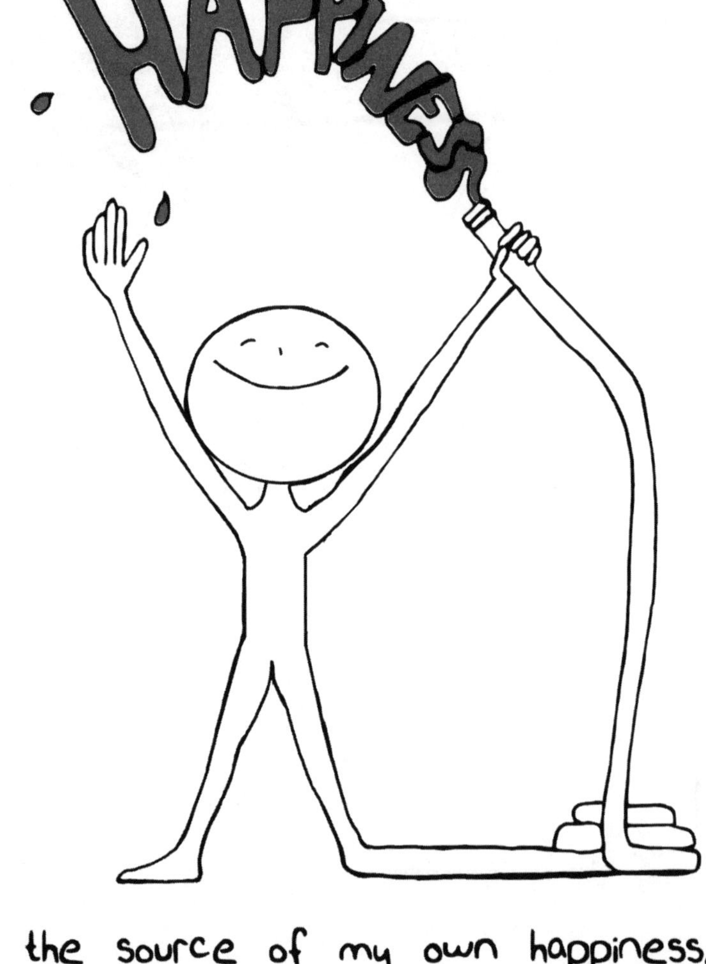
HAPPINESS

I am the source of my own happiness.

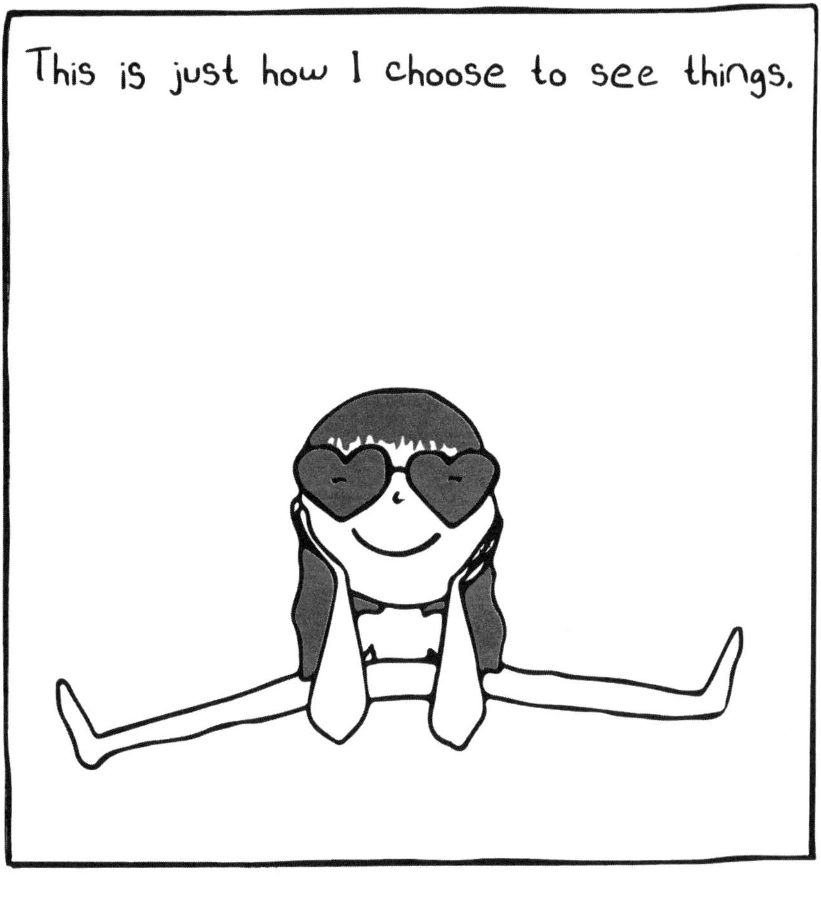
This is just how I choose to see things.

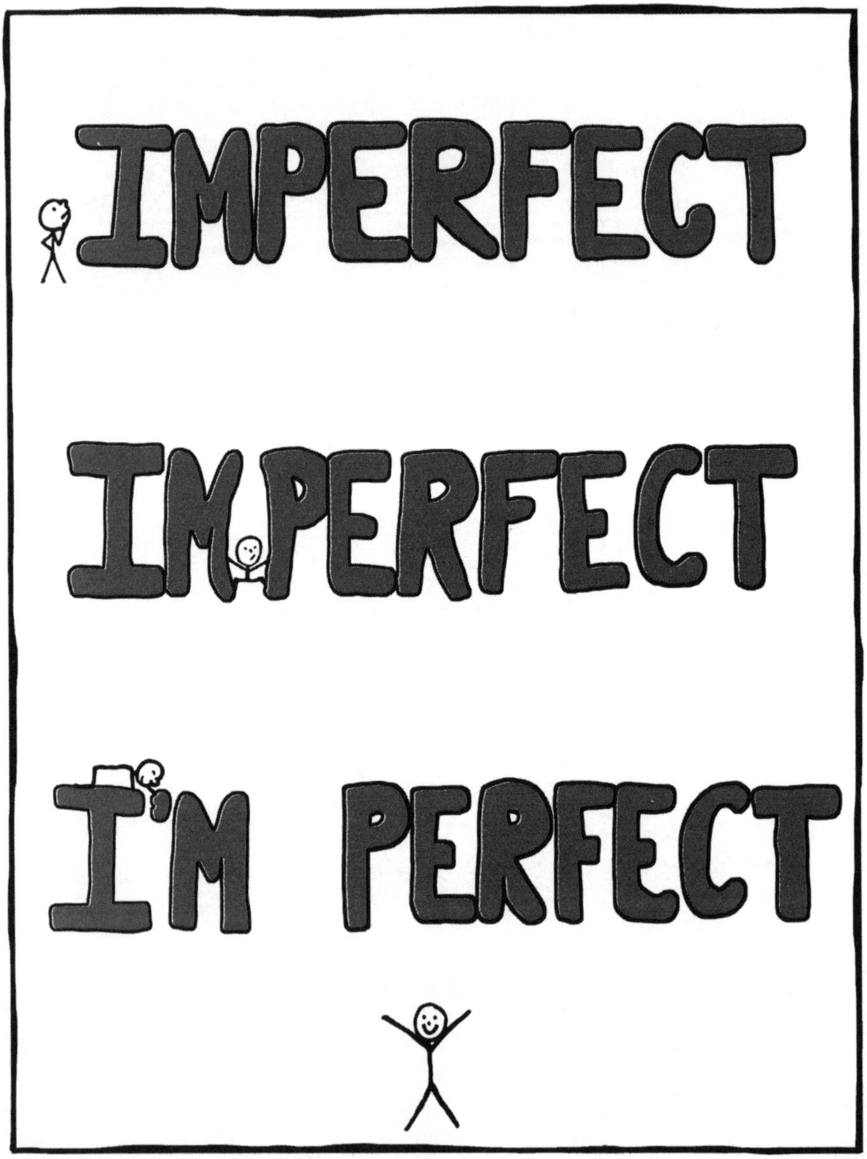
IMPERFECT
IM PERFECT
I'M PERFECT

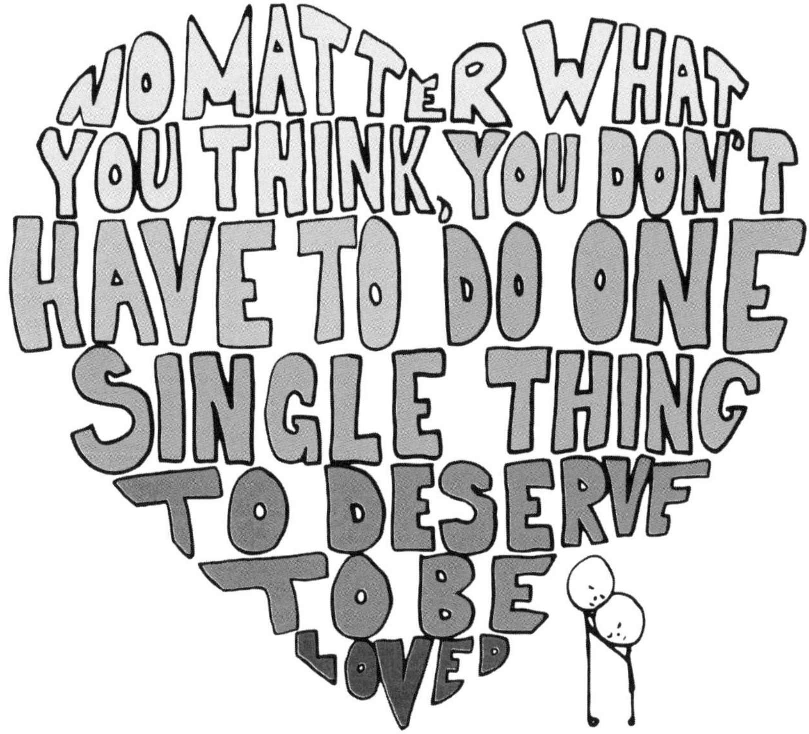
NO MATTER WHAT
YOU THINK, YOU DON'T
HAVE TO DO ONE
SINGLE THING
TO DESERVE
TO BE
LOVED

Mood Swings

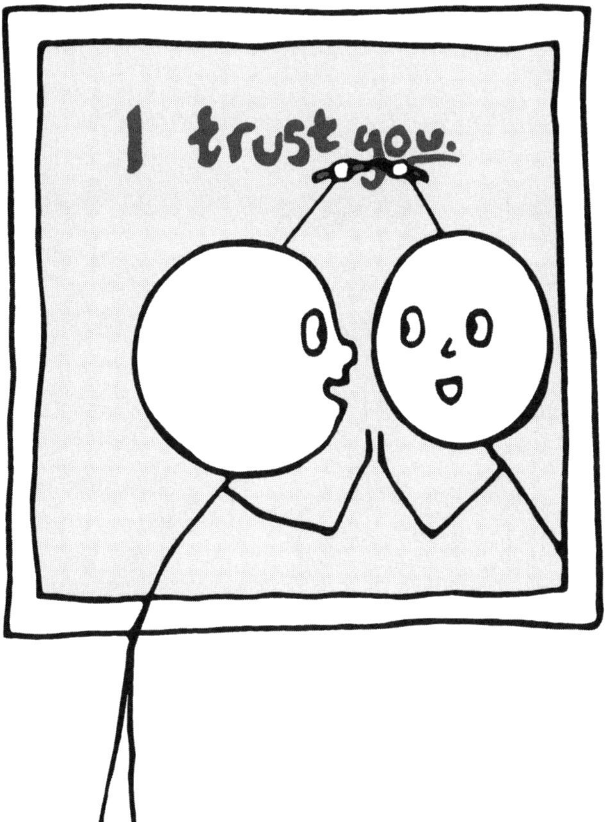
I trust you.

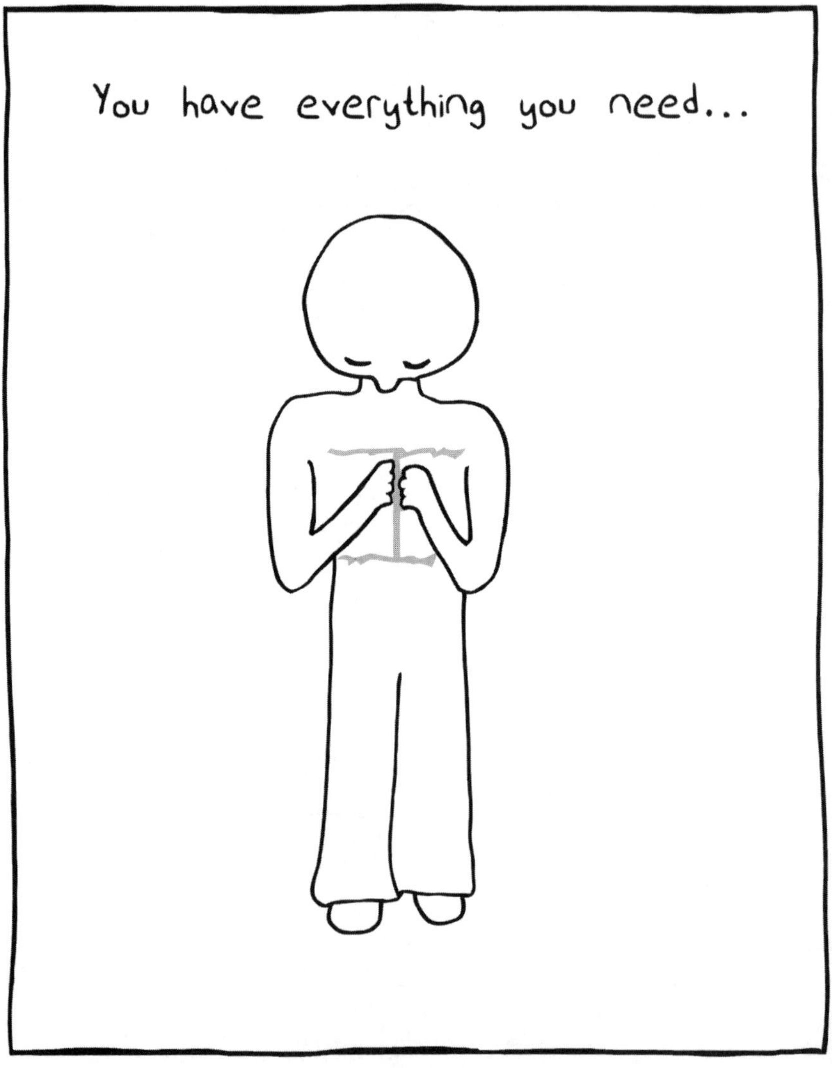
You have everything you need...

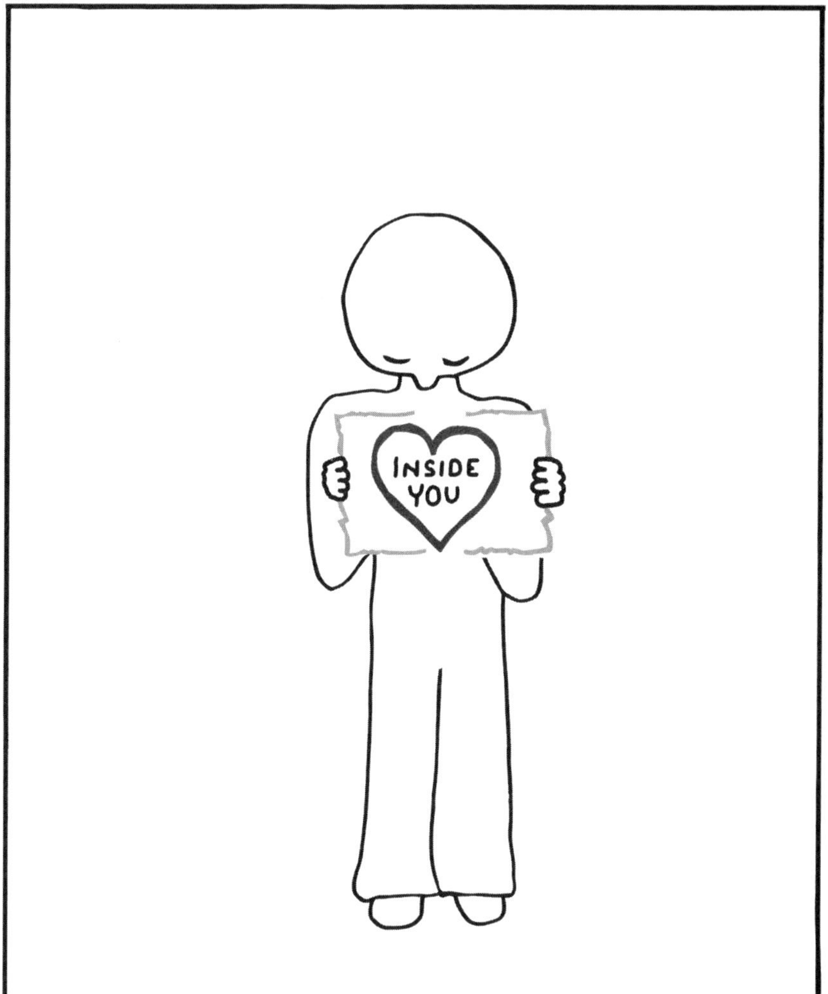
INSIDE
YOU

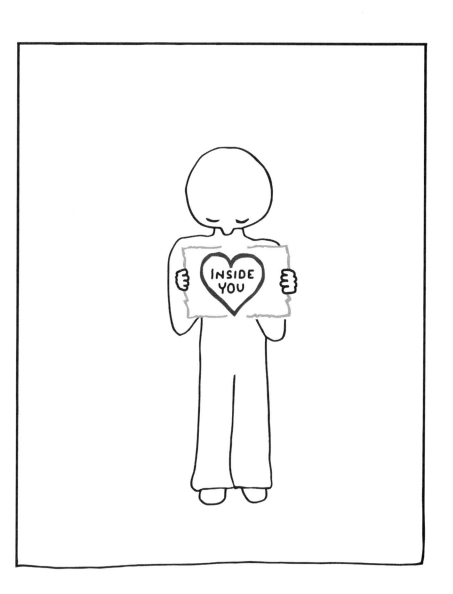

Two:

Loving You

The Way You Are

There's nothing you have to do
And nothing you have to say
And nothing you have to be
And nothing you have to change.

You may think you need to
Be better somehow,
But to me, you are PERFECT
Just the way you are now.

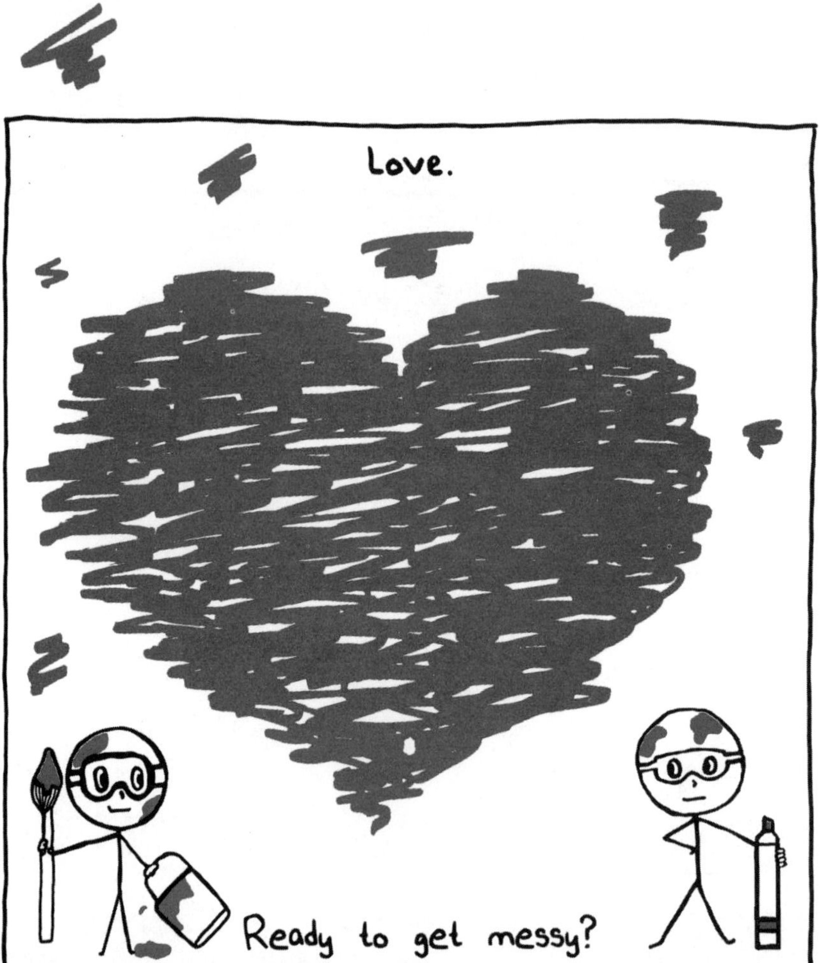
Love.
Ready to get messy?

When I think of you...

...my heart expands.

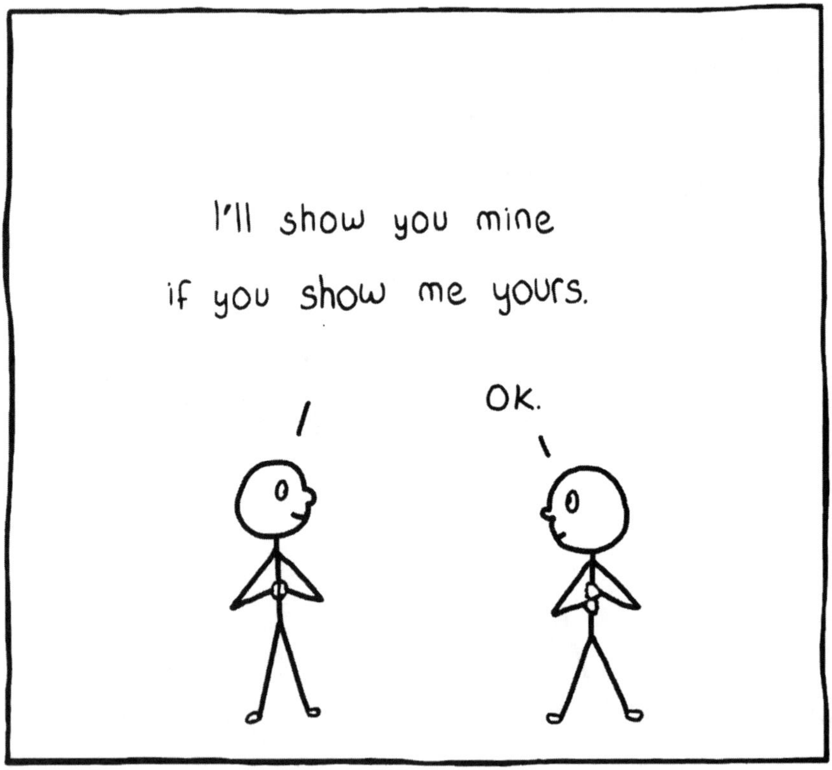
I'll show you mine
if you show me yours.
OK.

You cover the world in kindness.

You're worth figuring out.

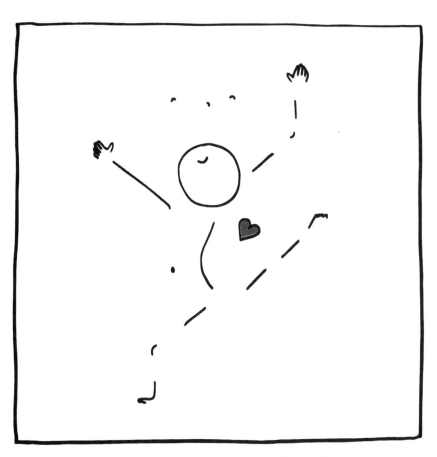

I love all your scattered parts.

mmmphhlepm.

grrrrr!

arrrgh!

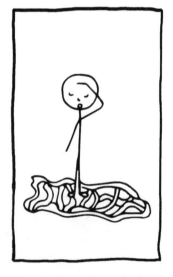

pheww ...

... I love you!

(Sorry it took me so long.

I had some stuff to work through.)

"Thank you for SHOWING UP and being

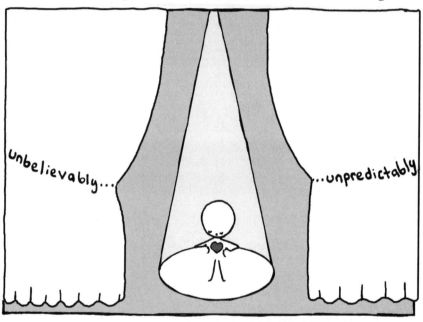

unbelievably... ...unpredictably

authentic." —Keah Kalantari

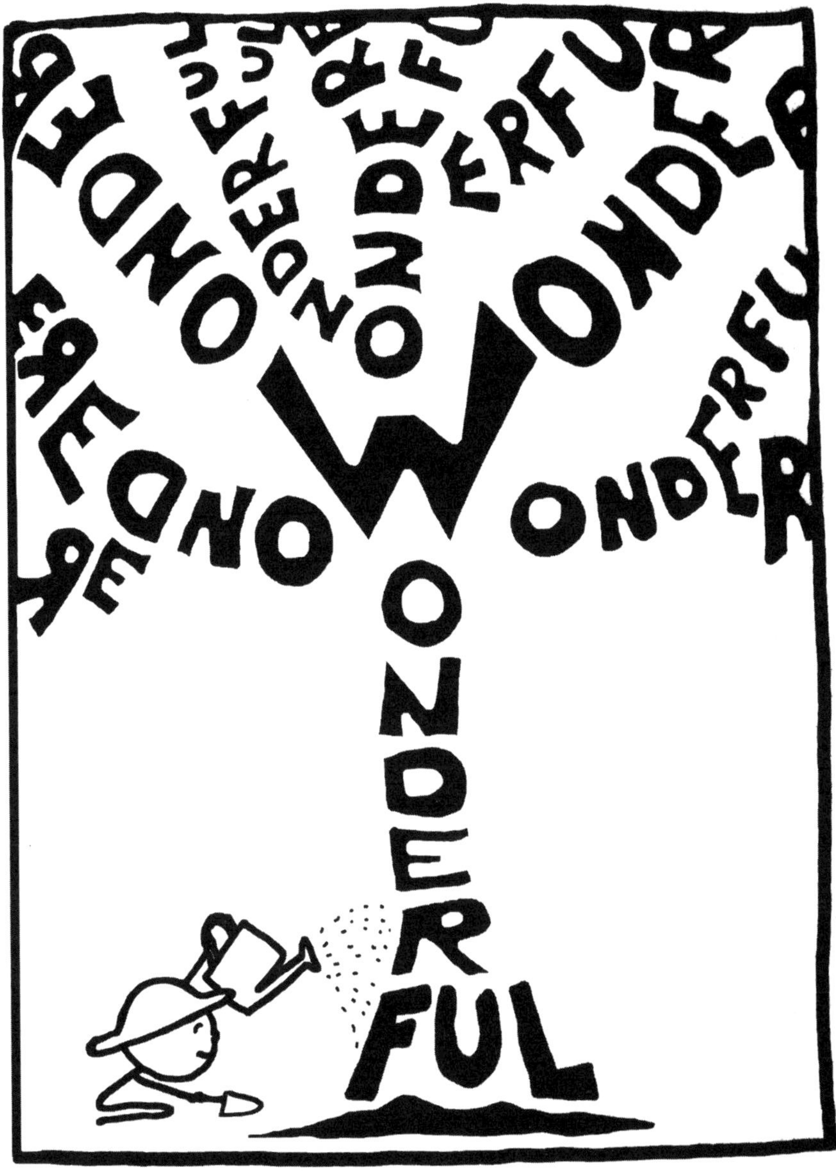
WONDERFUL

You keep growing more and more wonderful.

You inspire me.

You are absurdly sweet.

You make my heart race.

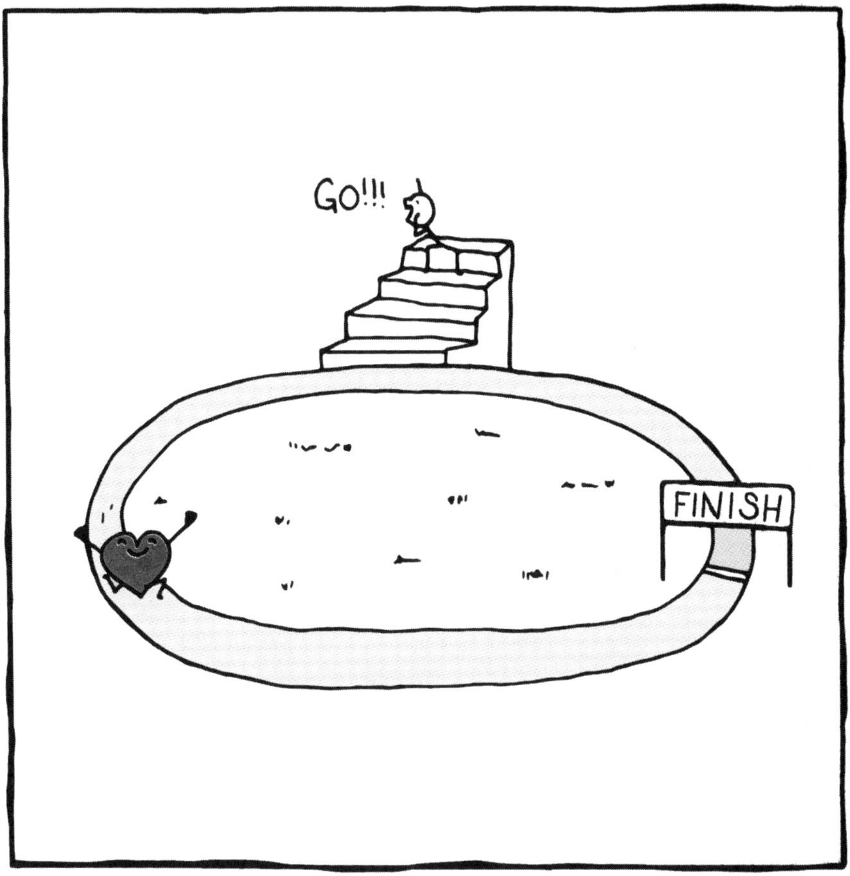
GO!!!
FINISH

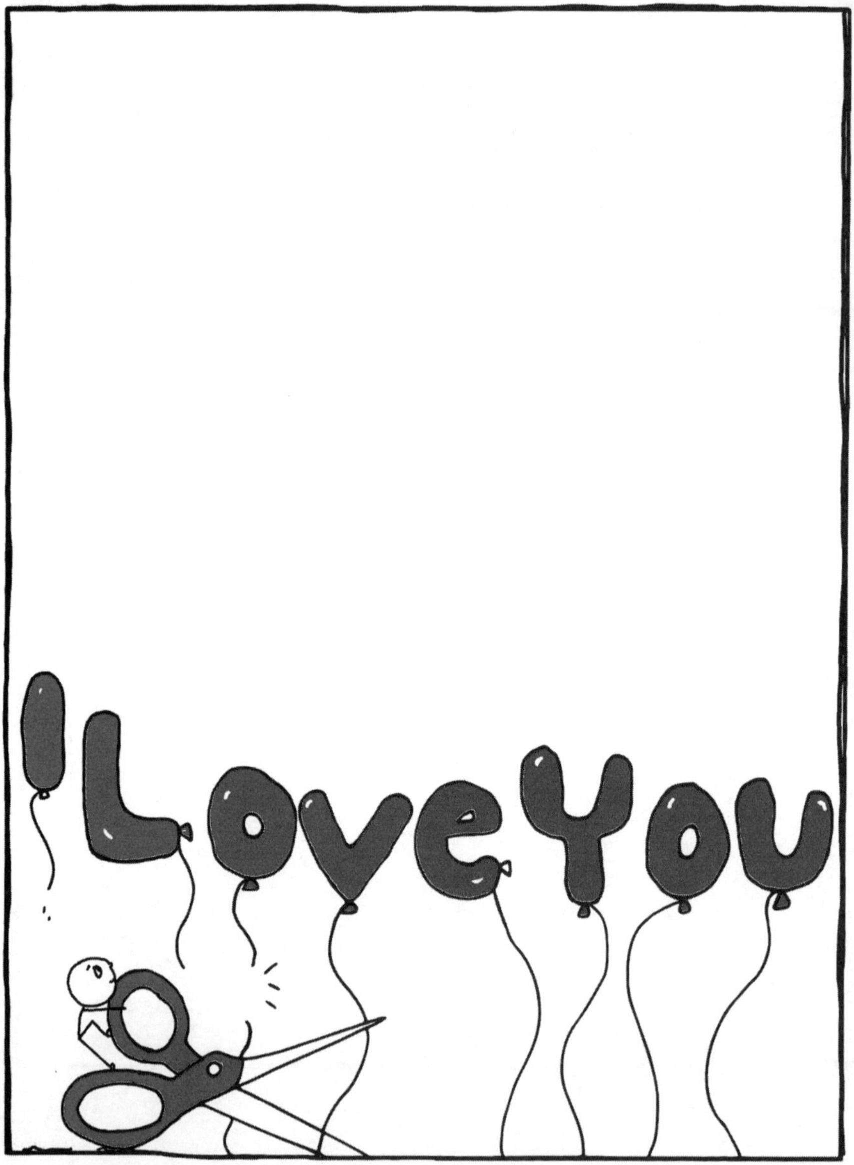
I Love You

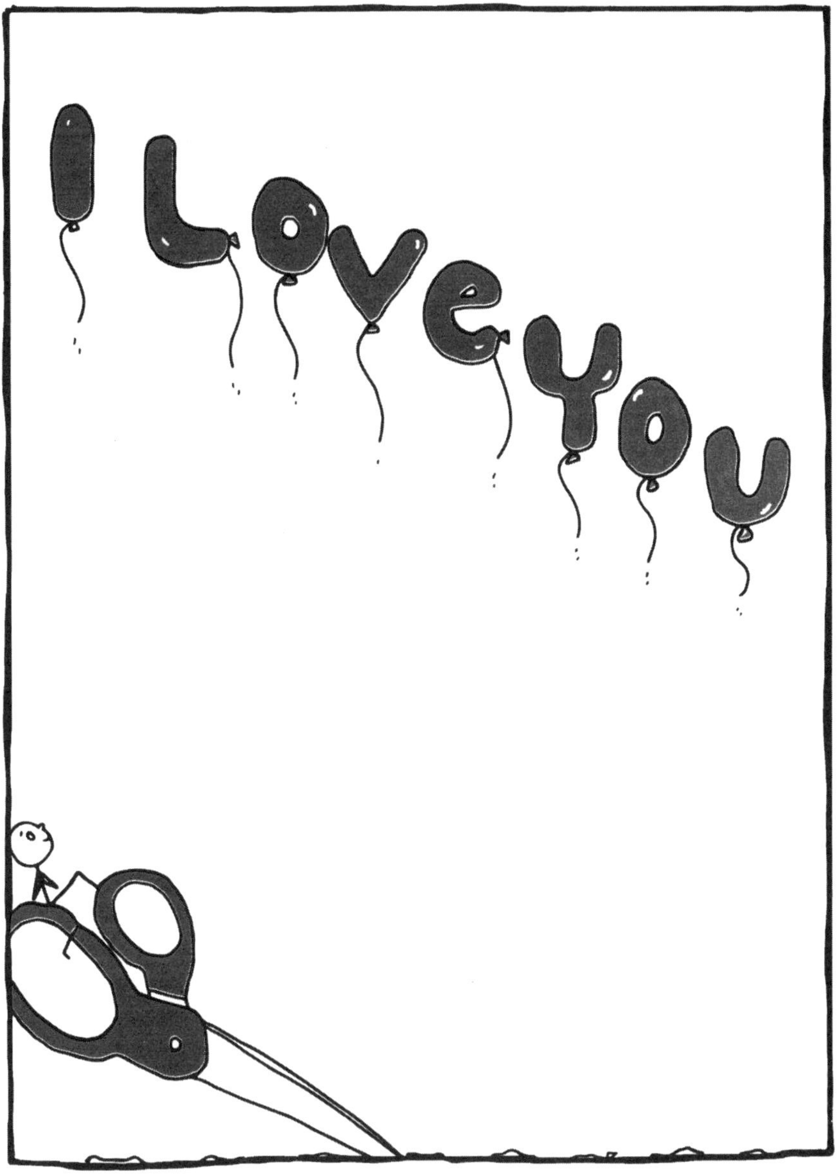
I LOVE YOU

no strings attached.

I just calculated...

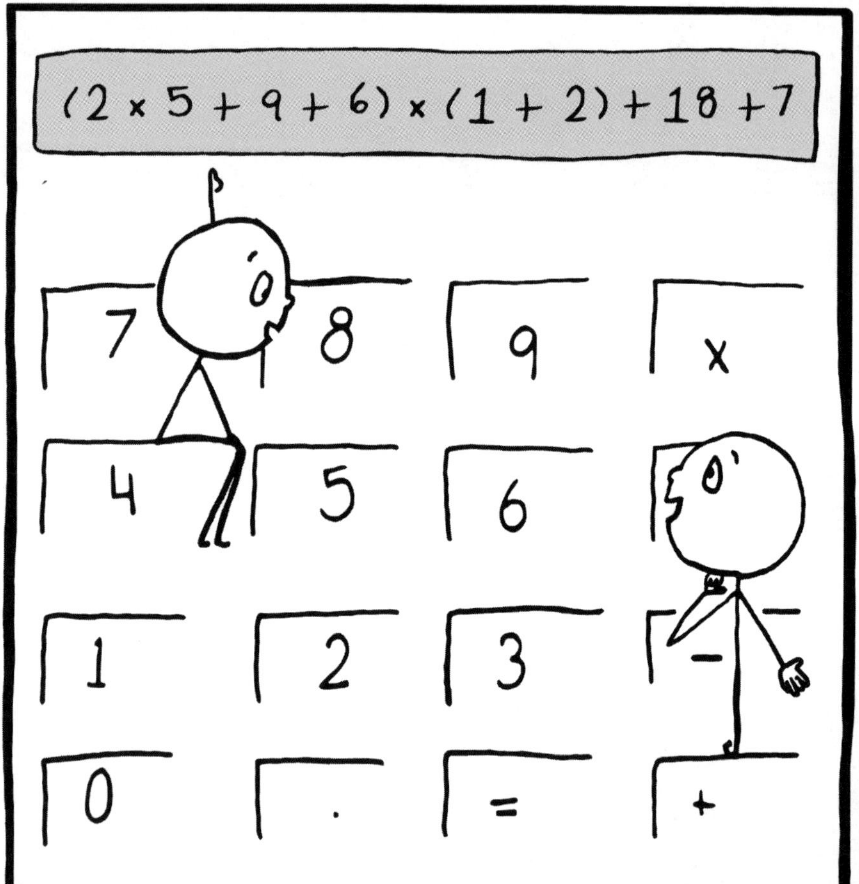
(2 x 5 + 9 + 6) x (1 + 2) + 18 + 7
7
8
9
x
4
5
6
1
2
3
–
0
.
=
+

...my life is 100% better with you in it.

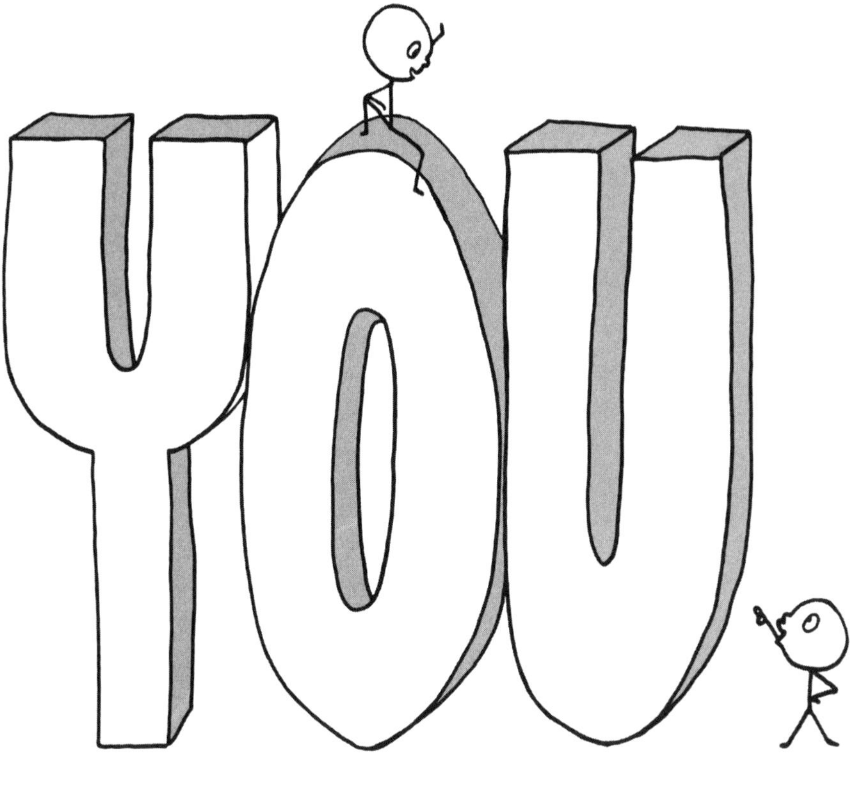
YOU.

always exceed my expectations.

In case it wasn't obvious...

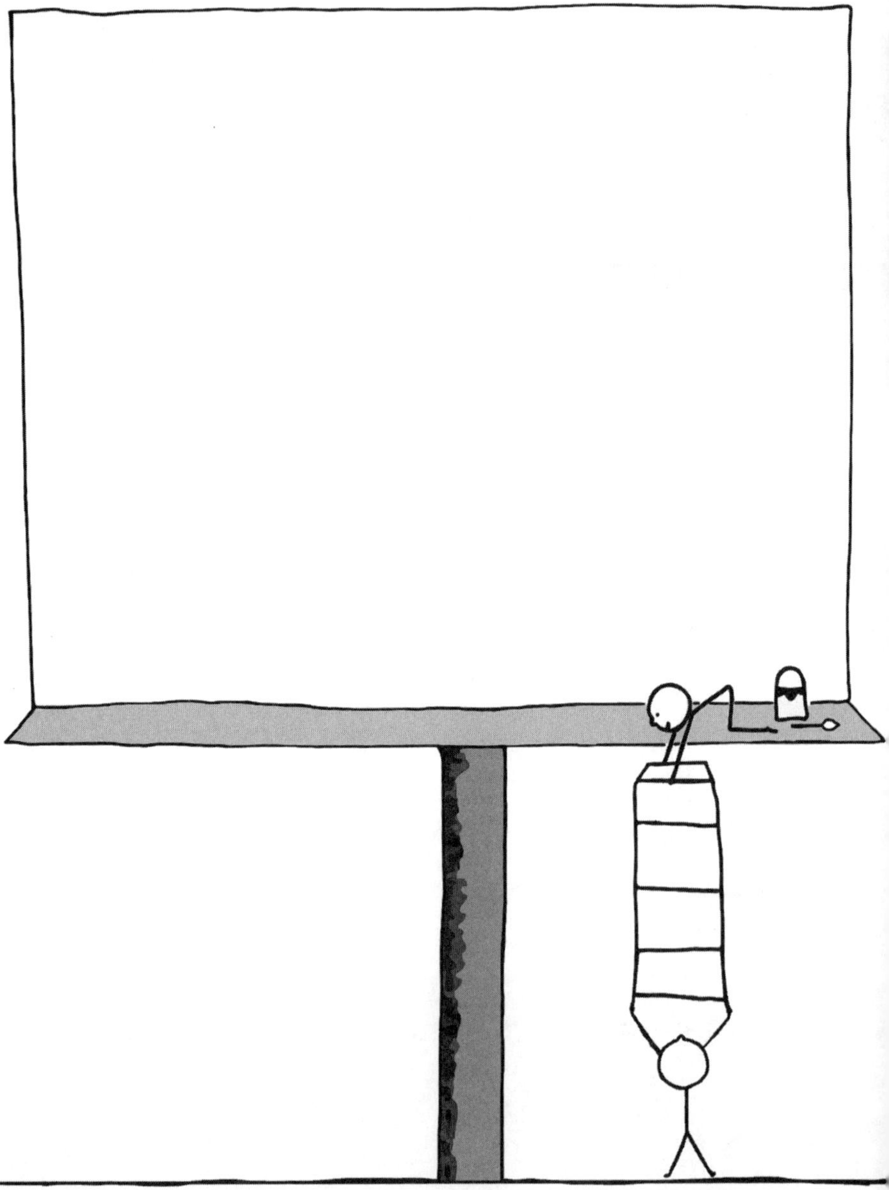

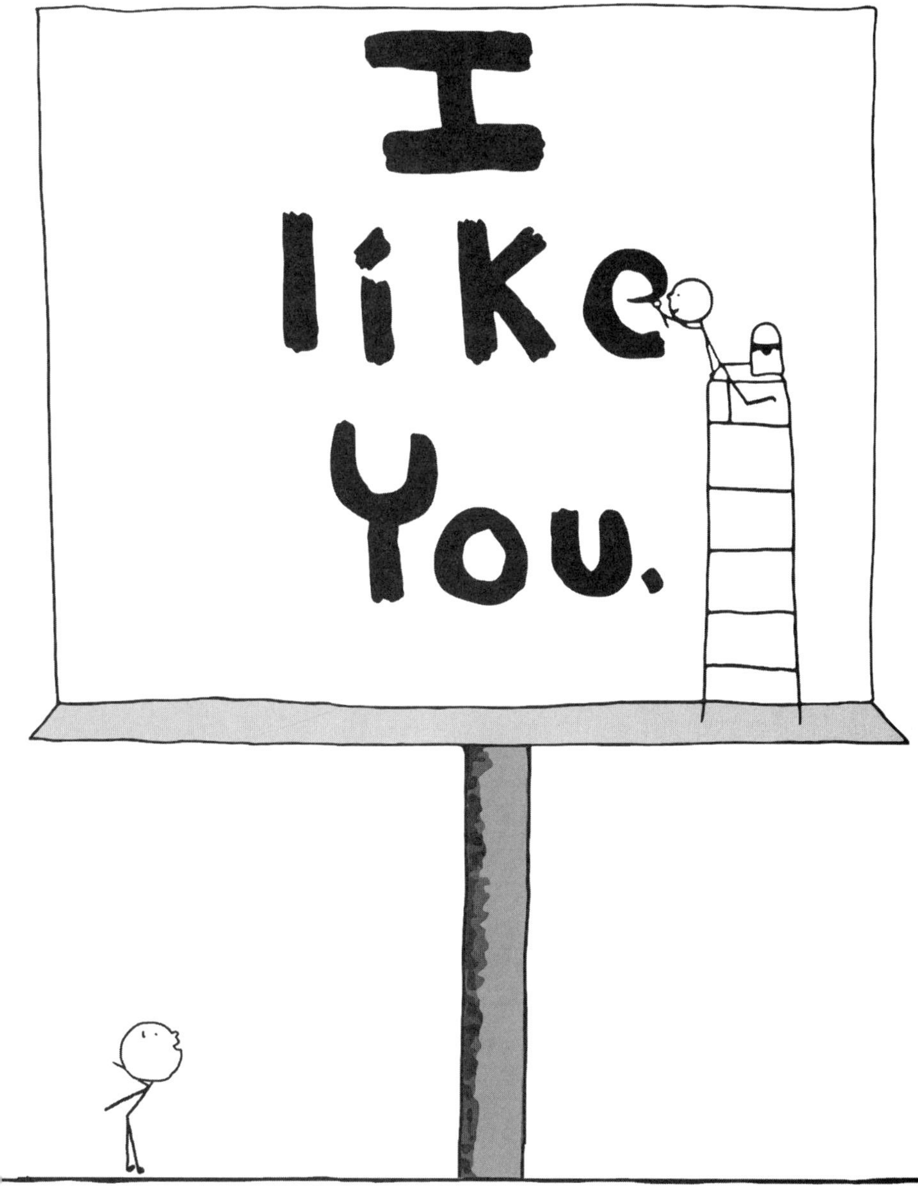
I like You.

Smitten Kitten

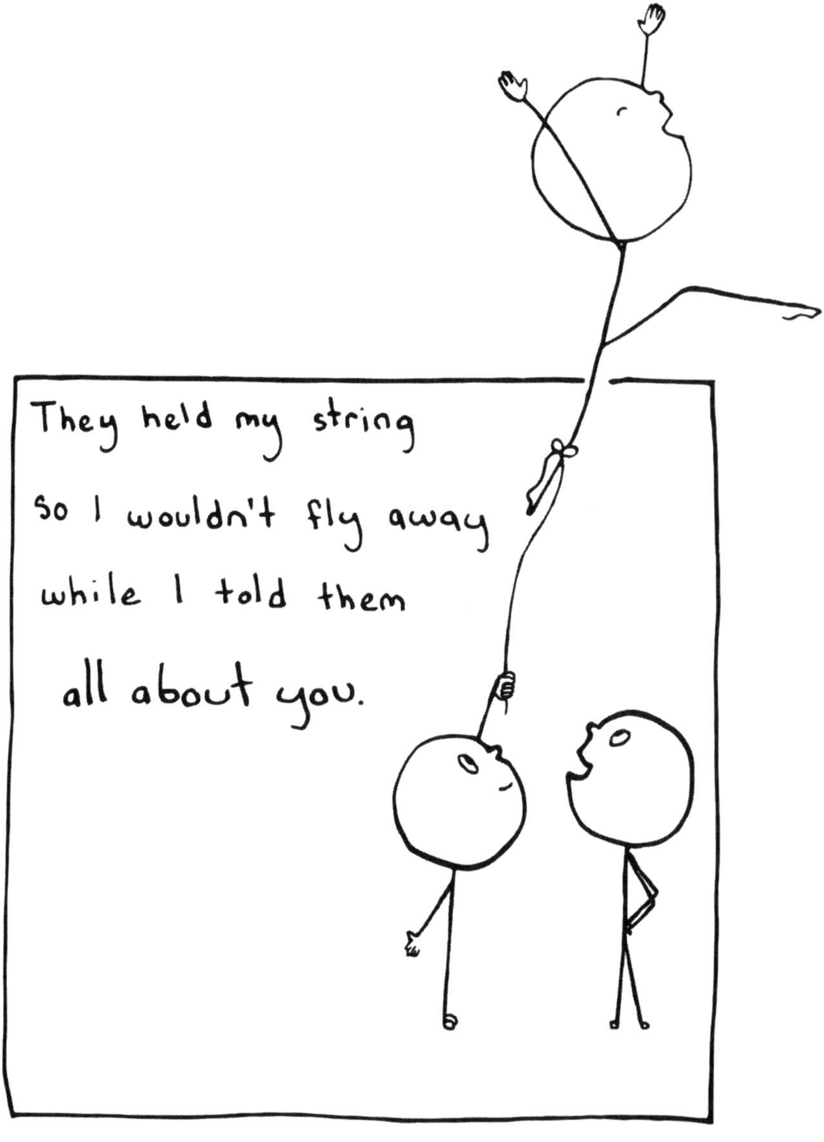
They held my string
so I wouldn't fly away
while I told them
all about you.

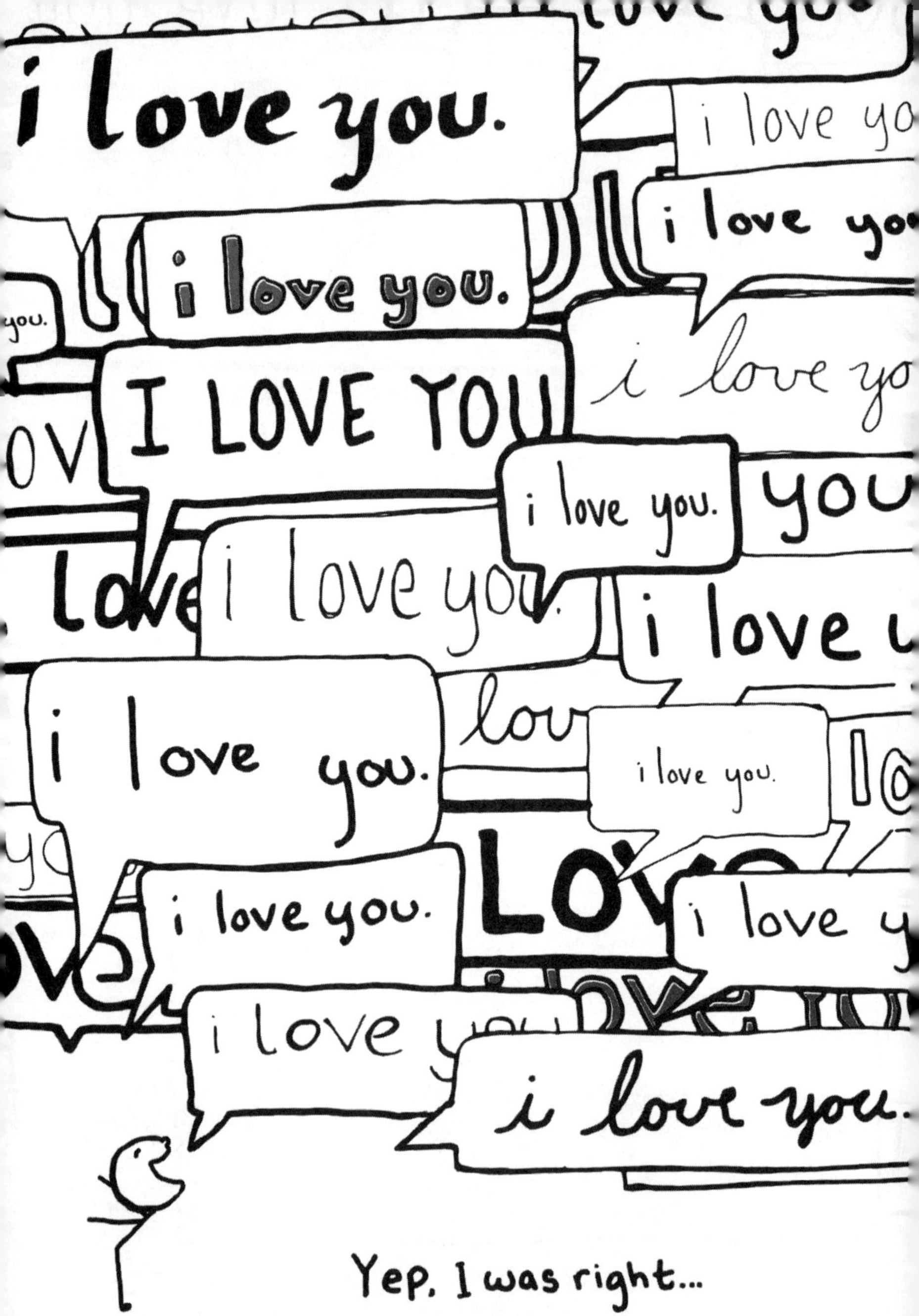
i love you.
i love yo
i love yo
you.
i love you.
I LOVE YOU
i love yo
i love you.
YOU
i love you
i love
i love you.
i love you.
LOV
i love
i love
i love you.
Yep. I was right...

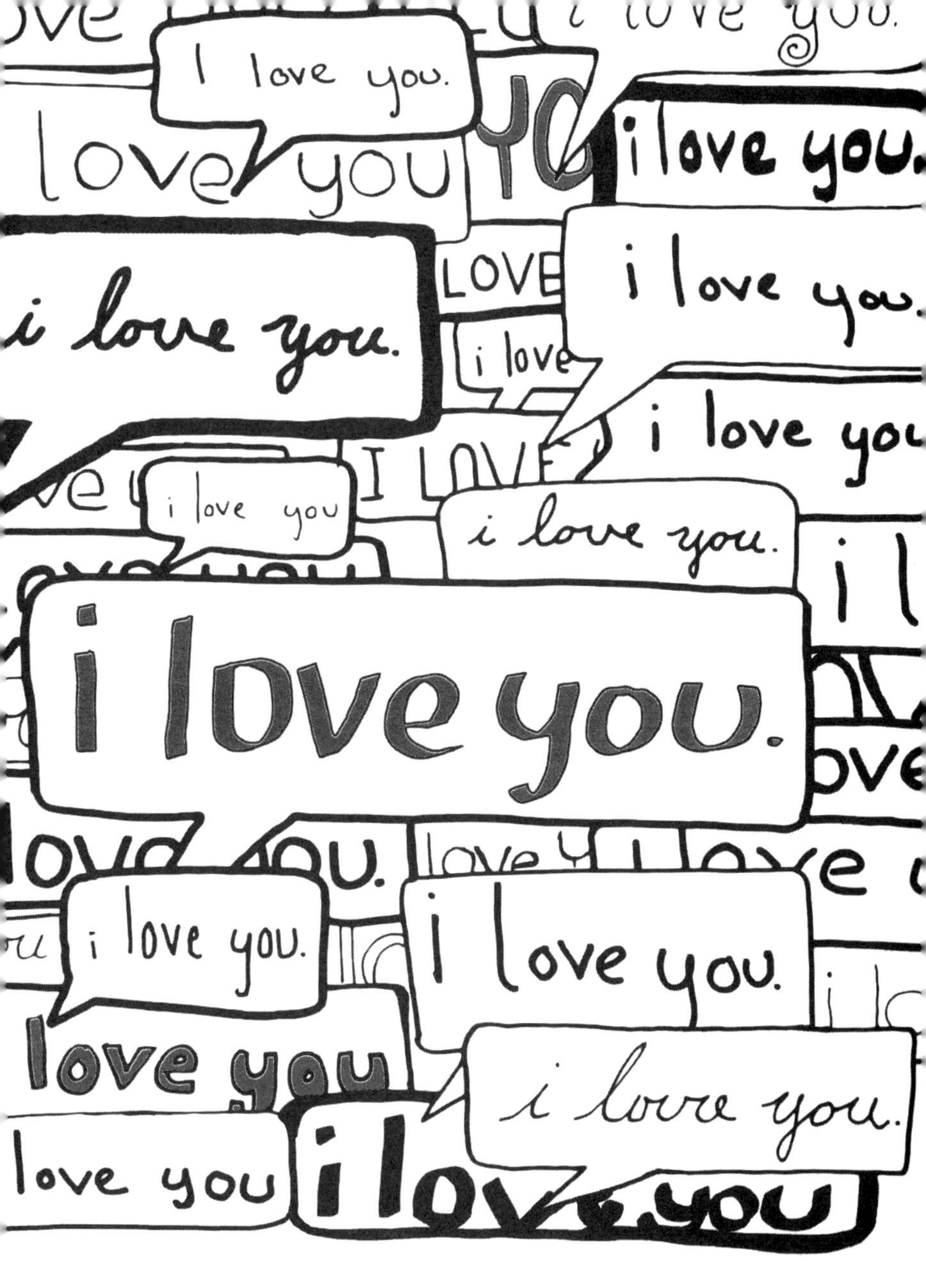
I love you.
love you
i love you.
LOVE
i love you.
i love you.
i love
i love you
i love you
i love you.
i love you.
i love you.
i love you.
love you
i love you.
love you
i love you

...I can't say it enough.

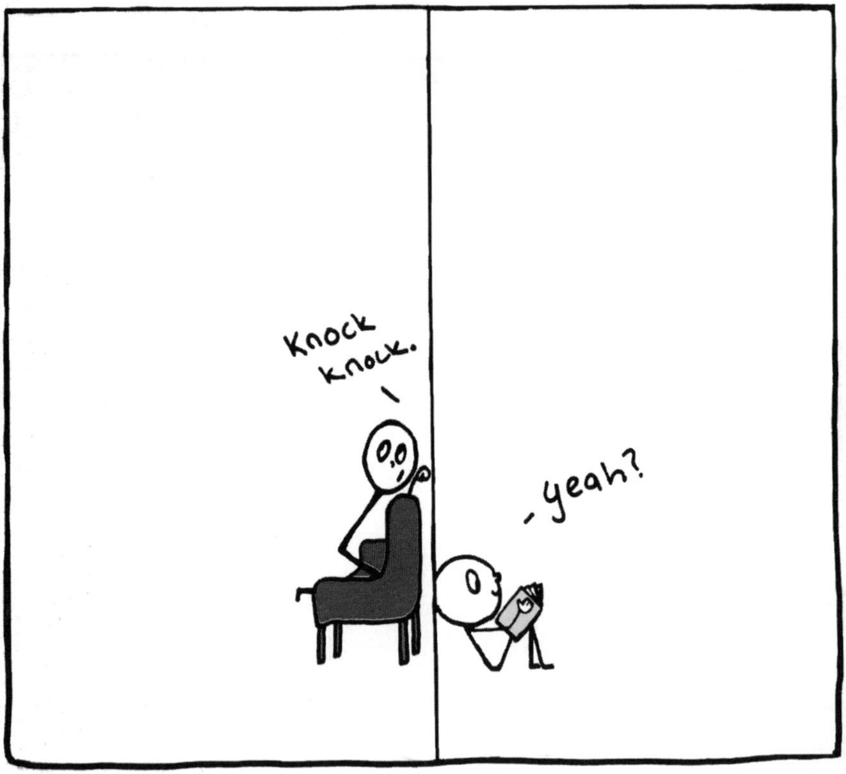
Knock knock.
-yeah?

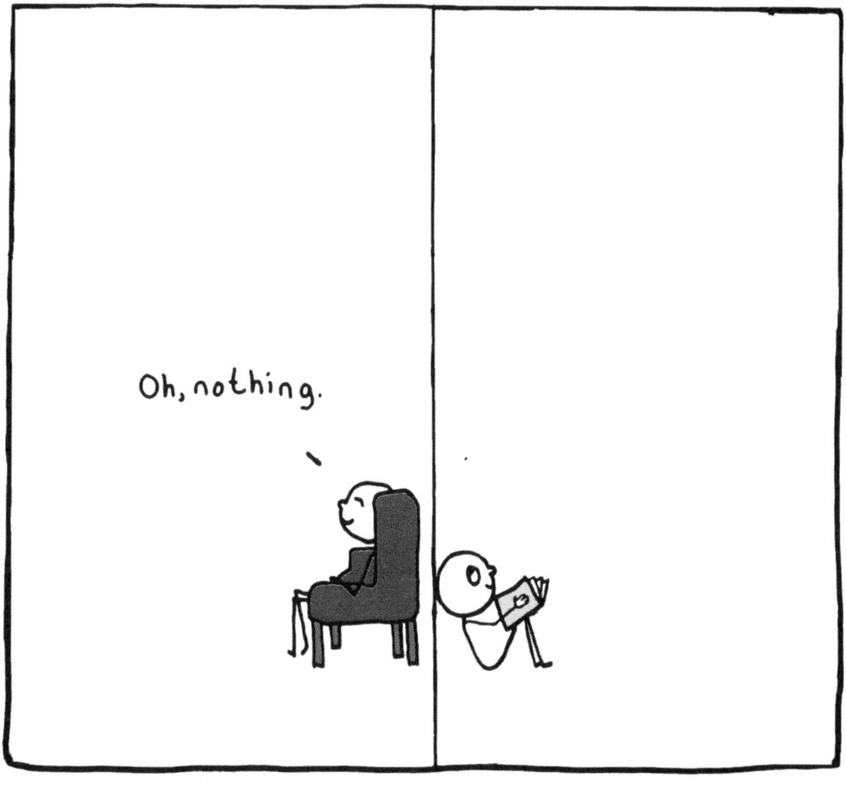
Oh, nothing.

(I just like knowing you're close.)

Three:

When Life Gets Hard

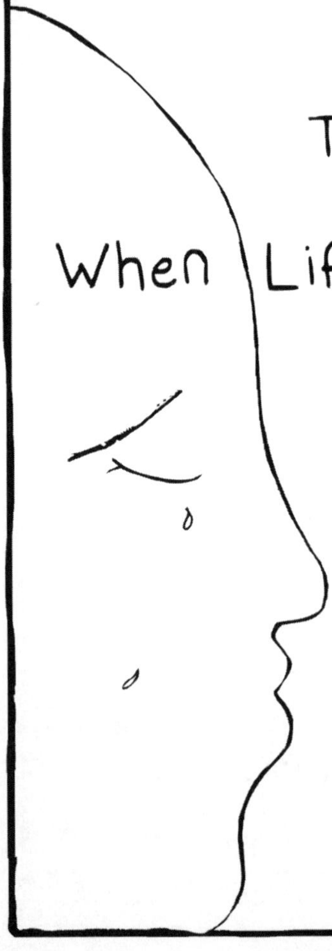

Whoever Told You

Whoever told you
    Not to be sad?
And whoever said
    That you shouldn't get mad?!
Whoever told you
    There's no need to cry?
And who said if you did
    That you need to know why?
Whoever said
    Not to feel what you feel?
And whoever said
    There's a right way to heal?
Whoever told you
    You need to be strong?
And whoever said
    That you're taking too long?
Whoever made you
    Doubt what you do?
Whoever knows anything
    Better than You?

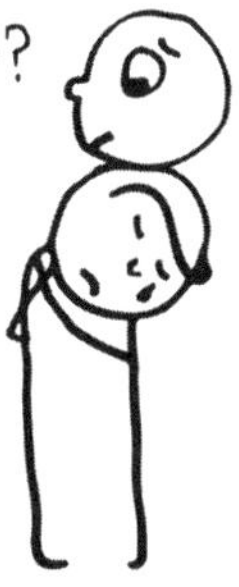

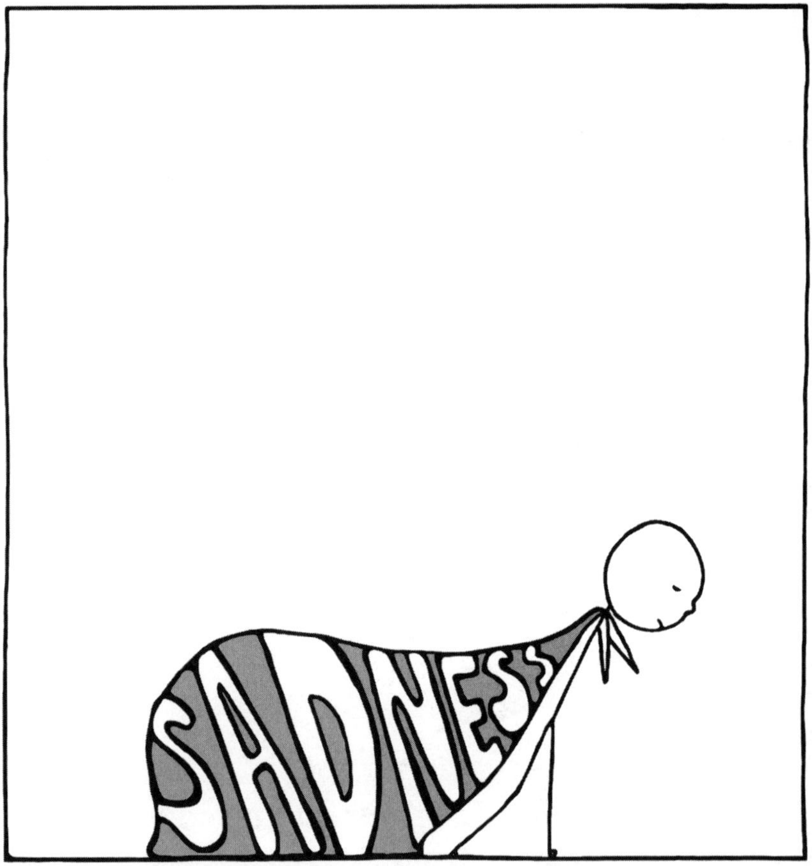
SADNESS

You don't have to carry this...

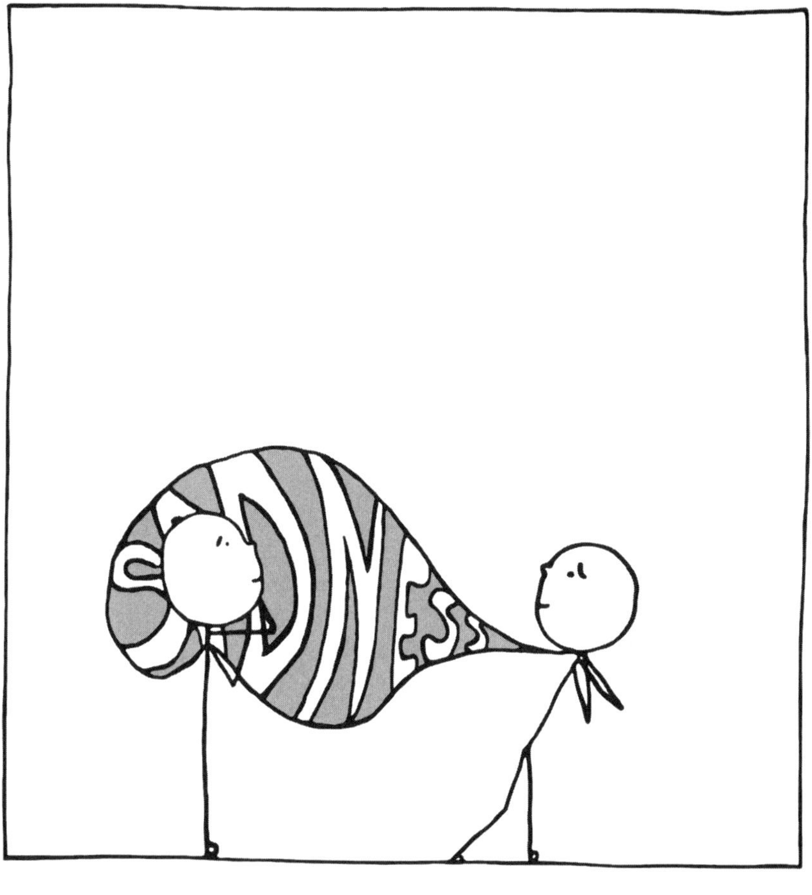

...alone.

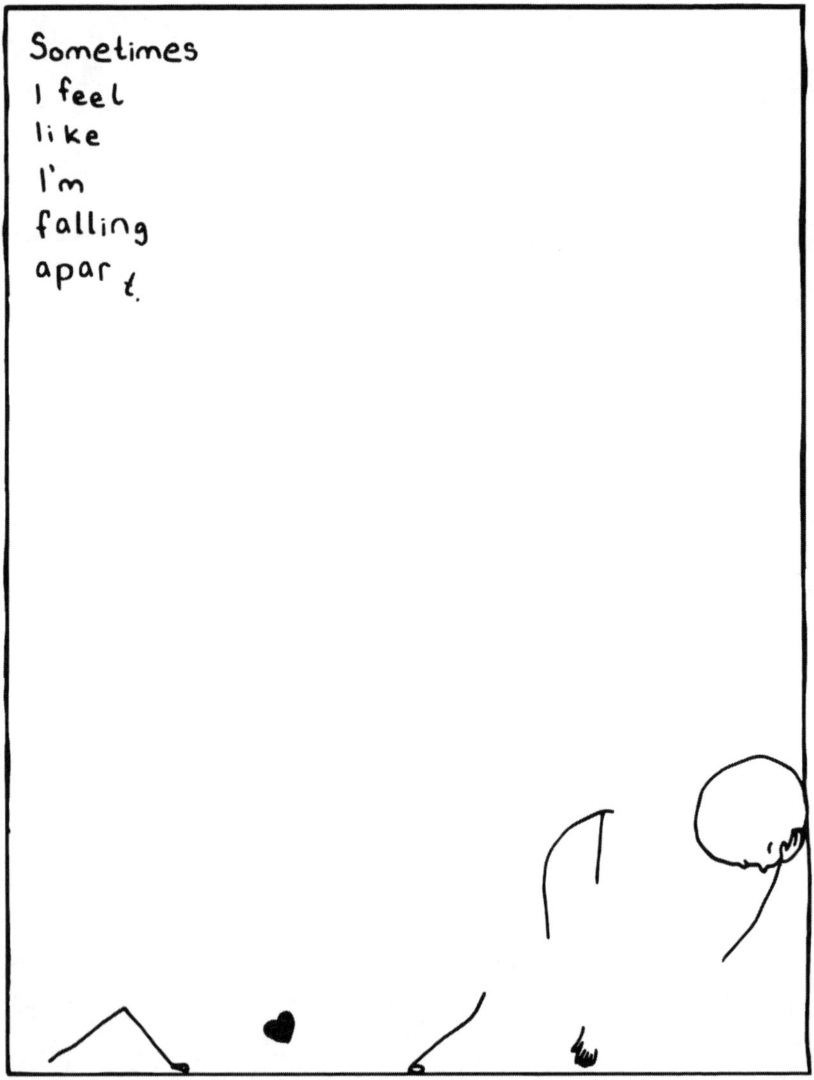
Sometimes
I feel
like
I'm
falling
apart.

Even when you're shattered, you're beautiful.

It won't hurt FOREVER...

...it just feels like it now.

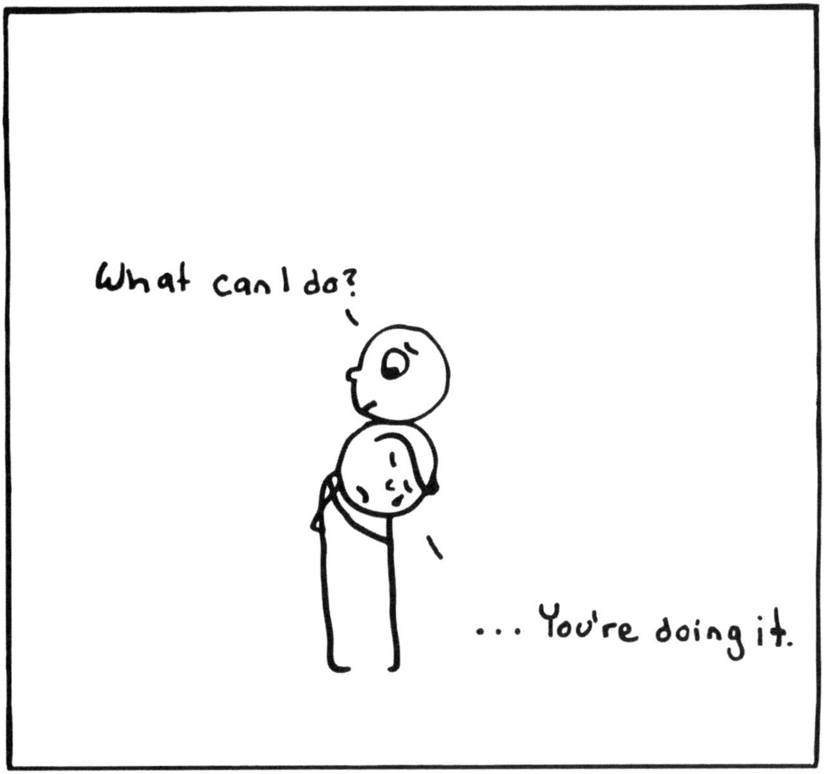
What can I do?
... You're doing it.

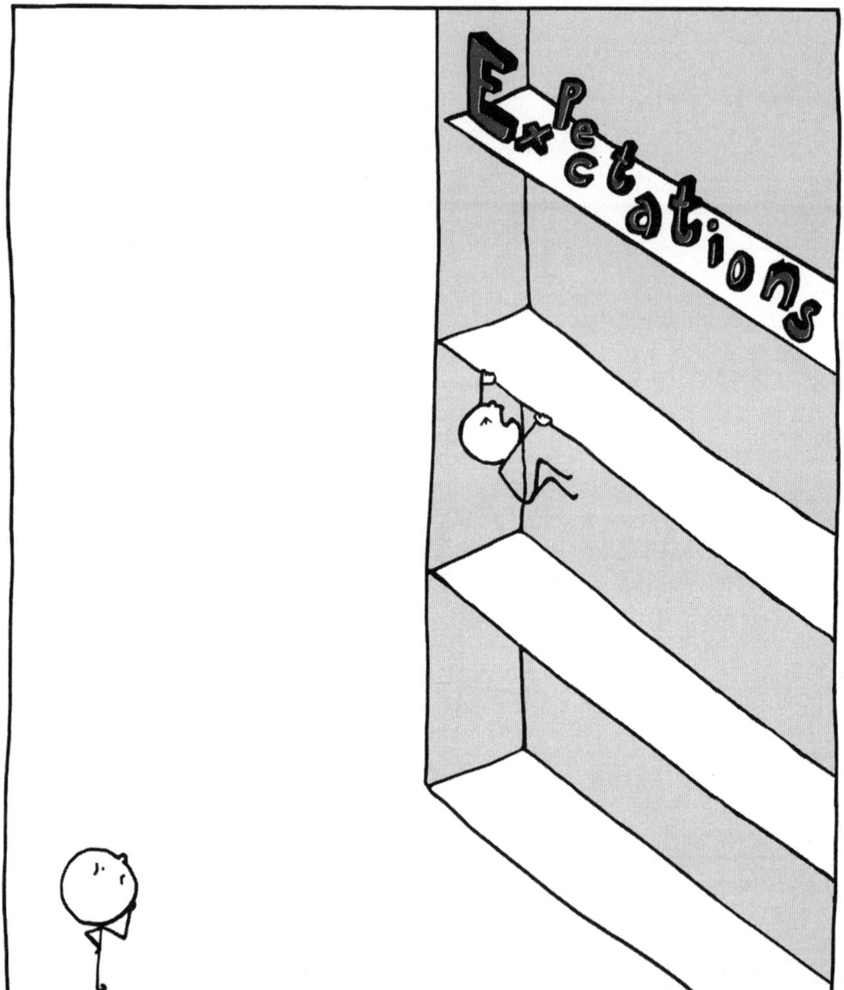
Expectations

You think maybe they're just too high?

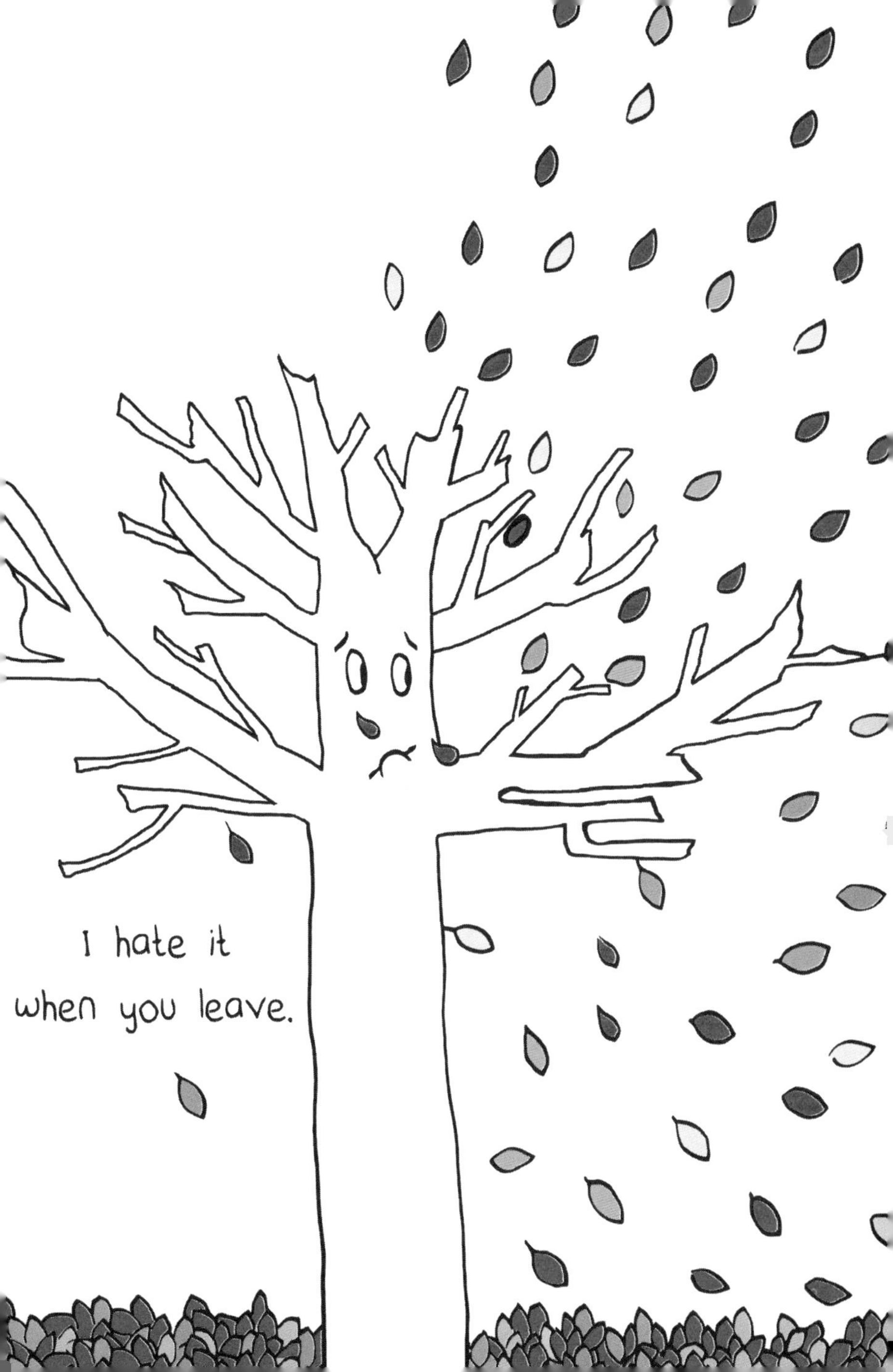
I hate it
when you leave.

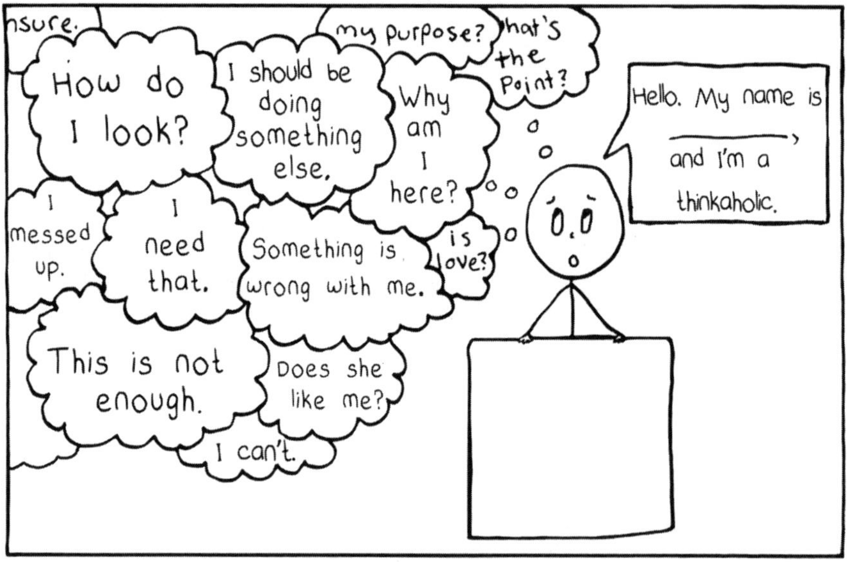
nsure.
my purpose?
hat's the Point?
How do I look?
I should be doing something else.
Why am I here?
I messed up.
I need that.
Something is wrong with me.
is love?
This is not enough.
Does she like me?
I can't.
Hello. My name is ________, and I'm a thinkaholic.

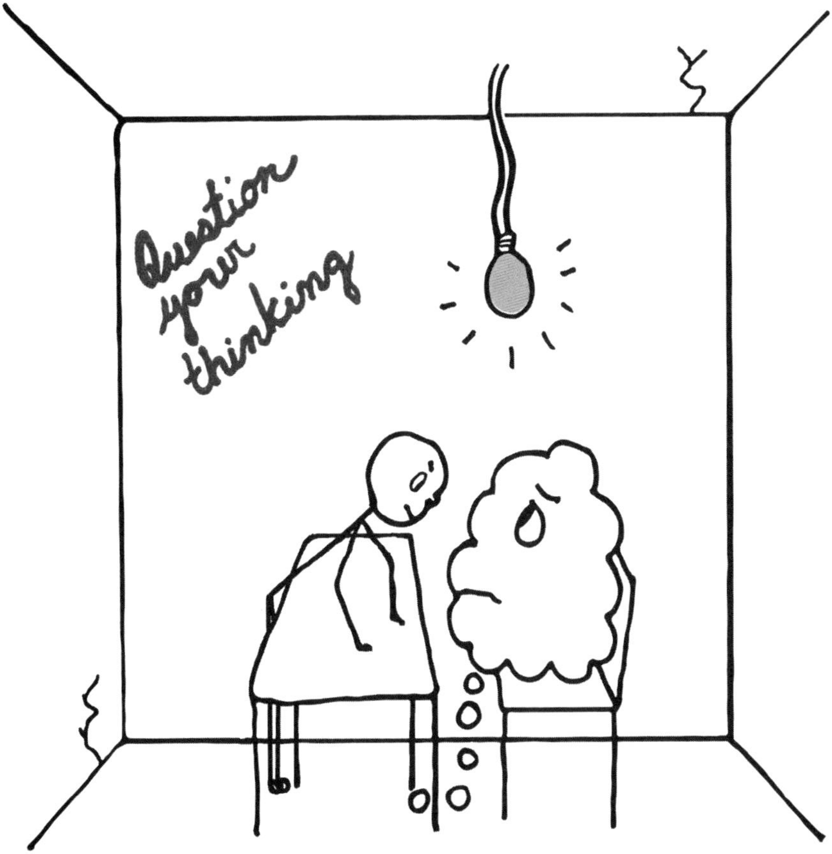
Question your thinking

Sometimes I get so lost in my head...

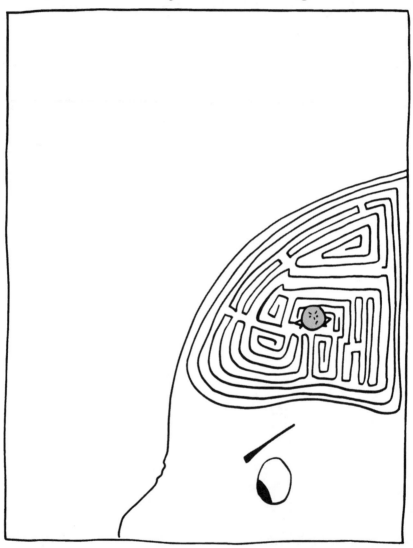

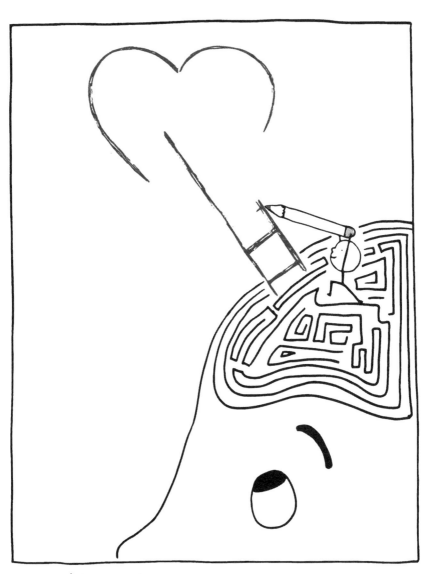

...I have to draw my way out.

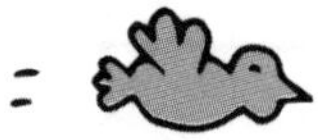

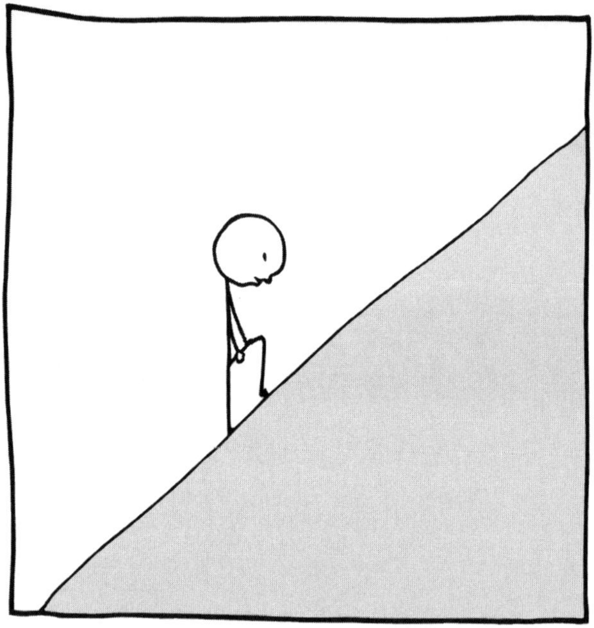

when life seems hard...

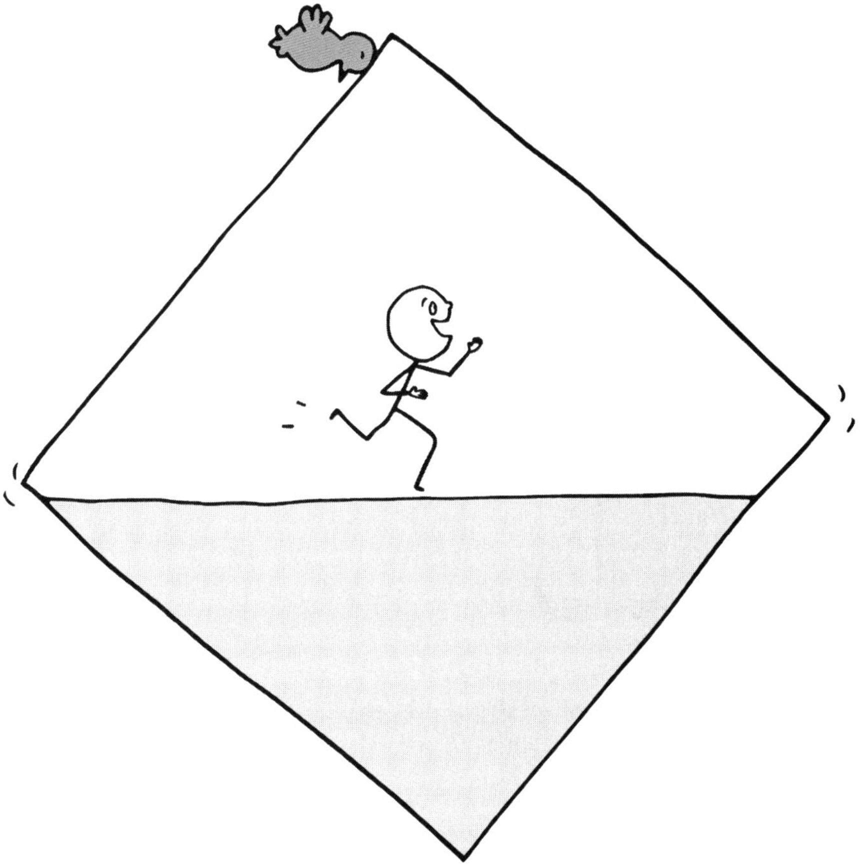

...try changing perspective.

Sometimes when I feel worthless...

...you make me feel priceless.

I miss you...

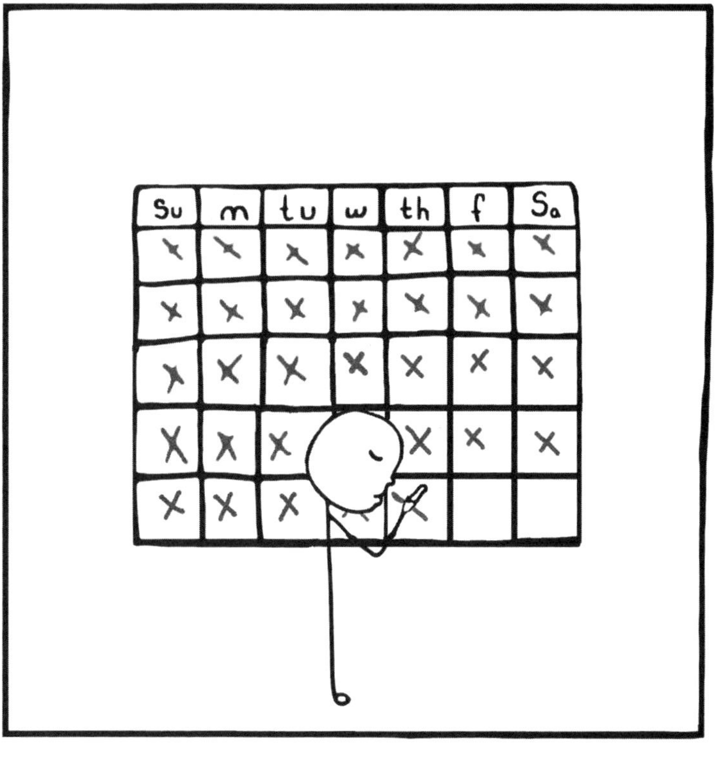
Su
m
tu
w
th
f
Sa

...every day.

Memory is time folding up...

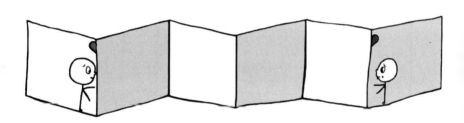

...so I can be near you again.

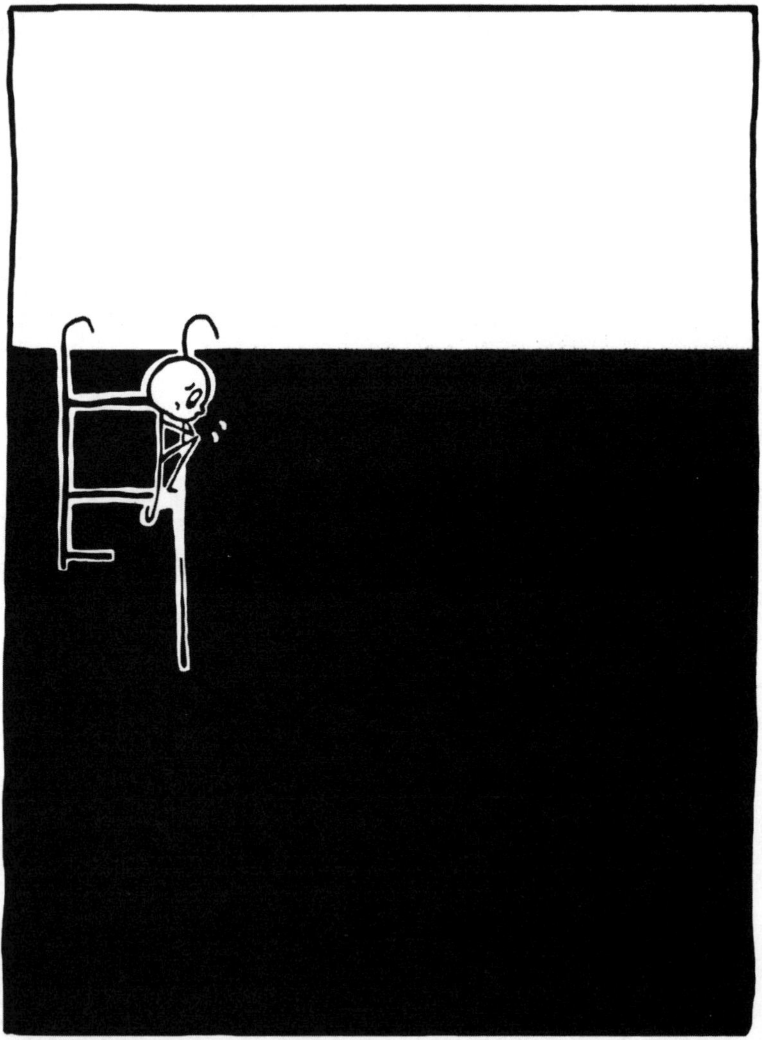

Sometimes you gotta go down...

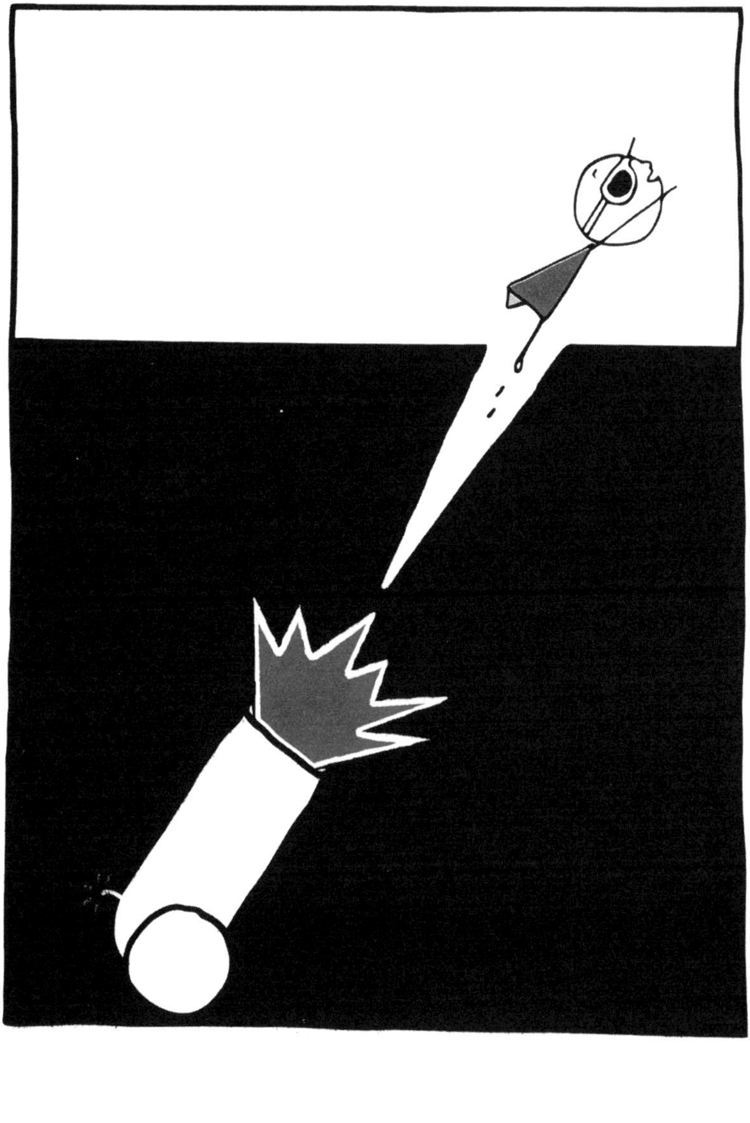

...before you come back up.

Don't worry!

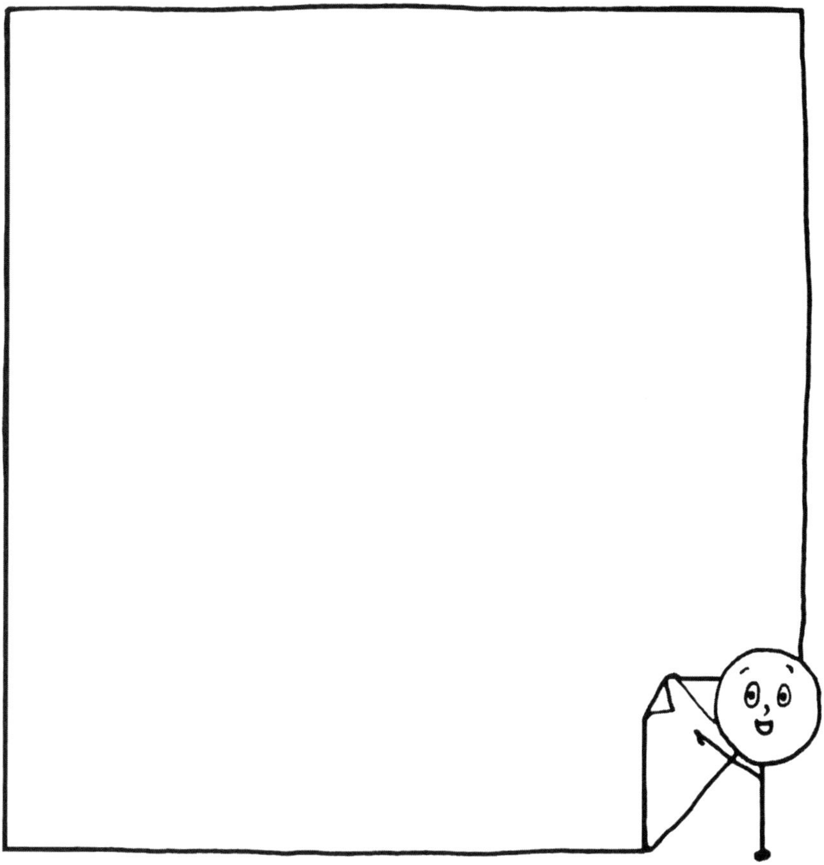

I'm in your corner.

The Elephant in the Room

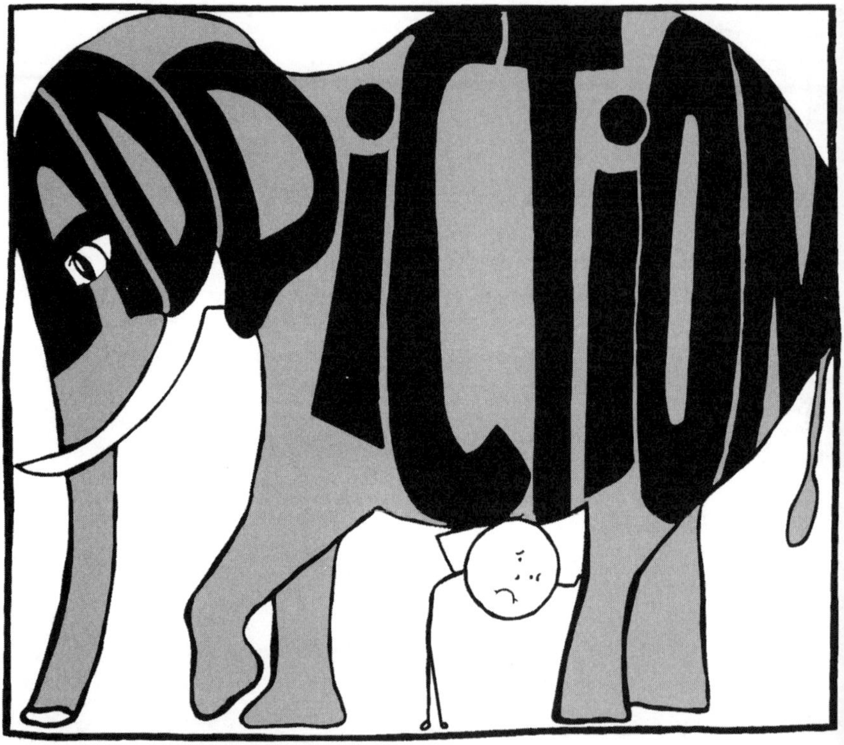
ADDICTION

"Don't worry, I think I've got it under control."

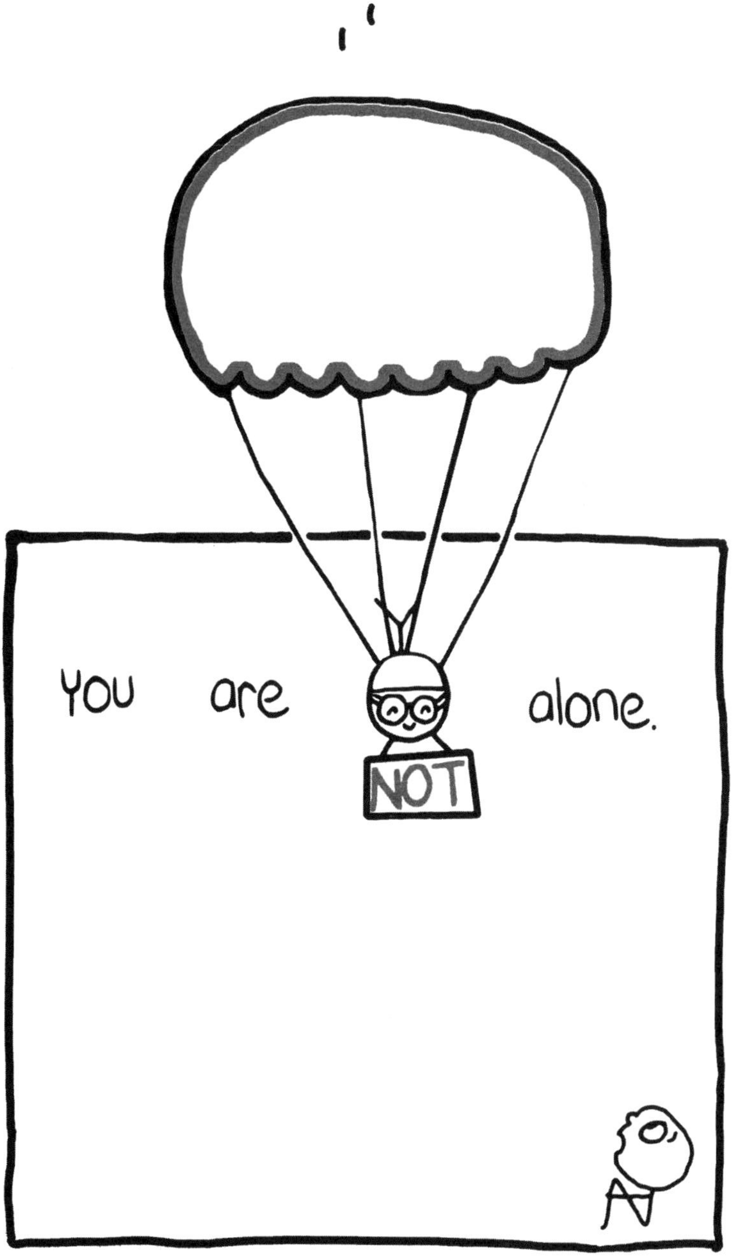
You are
NOT
alone.

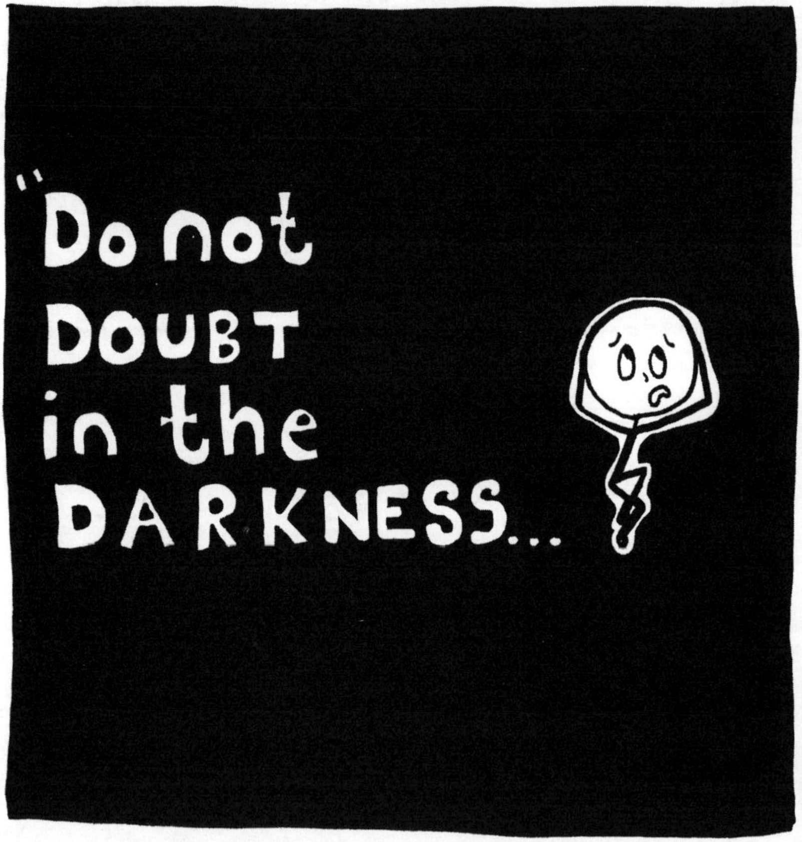
"Do not
DOUBT
in the
DARKNESS...

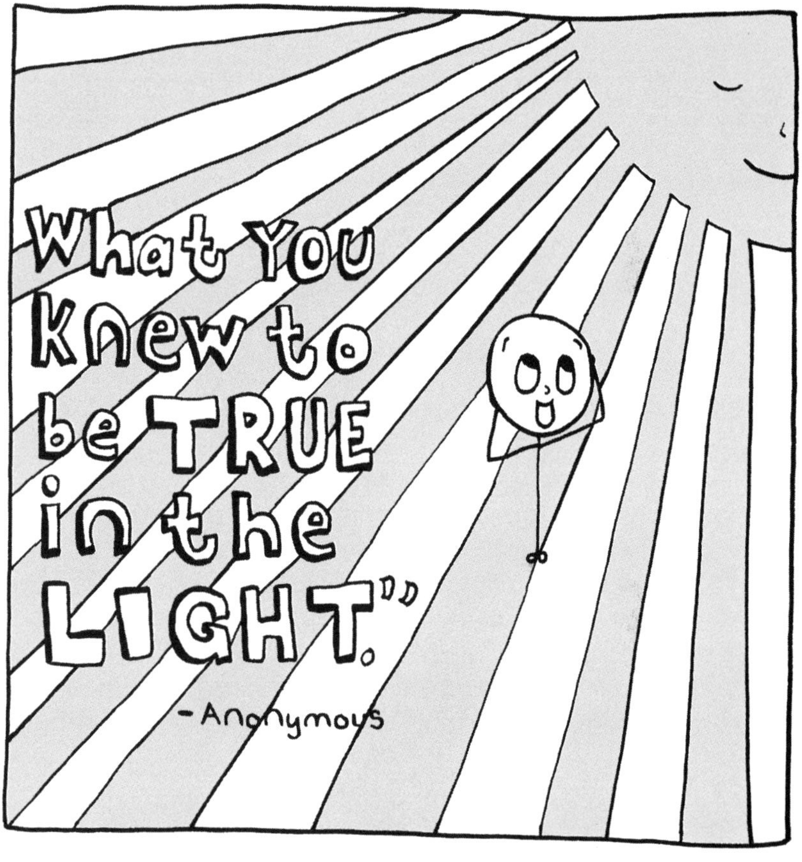
What You knew to be TRUE in the LIGHT."
-Anonymous

Four:

Choose Your Own Adventure

Tiny Little Yes

There's a tiny little YES inside
Hiding where the YESes hide.
You'll find it squeezed in right beside
A MAYBE and a CAN'T-DECIDE.

It's buried down beneath the WOEs
Somewhere between the NAYs and NOs
You'll have to look past rows and rows
Of SORT OFs, NOT QUITES and SO-SOs.

Once your YES is in your grasp
Prepare to wonder, gape and gasp.
You may suspect, "This can't be right!"
But trust your gut and hold on tight.

un...

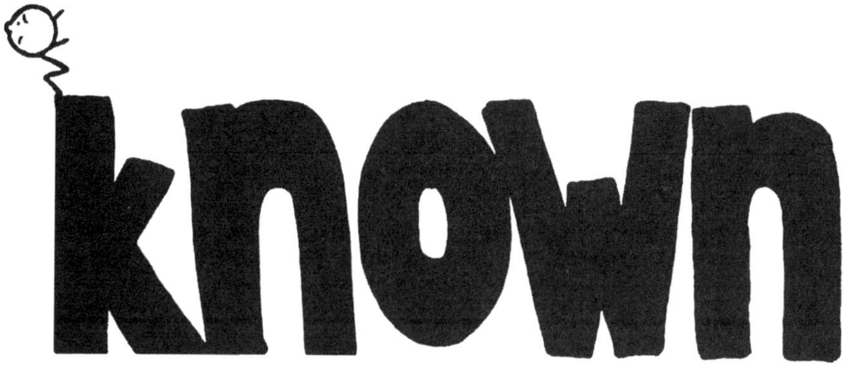
known

My goodness, that's a big leap!

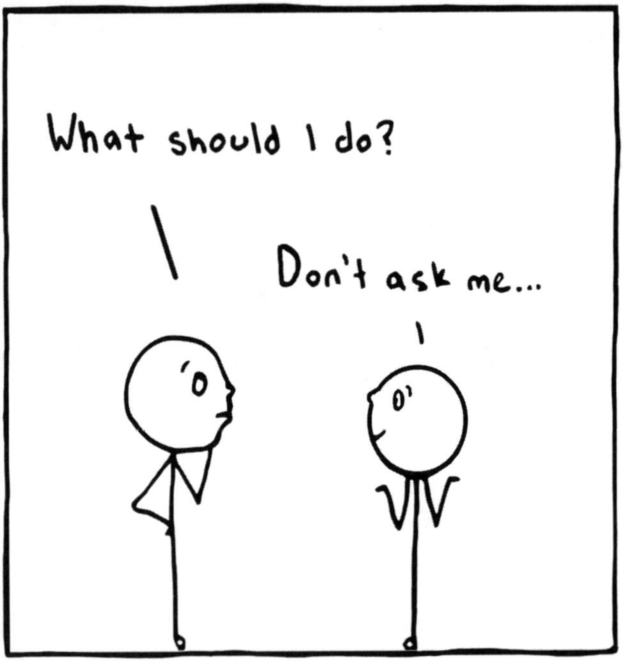
What should I do?
Don't ask me...

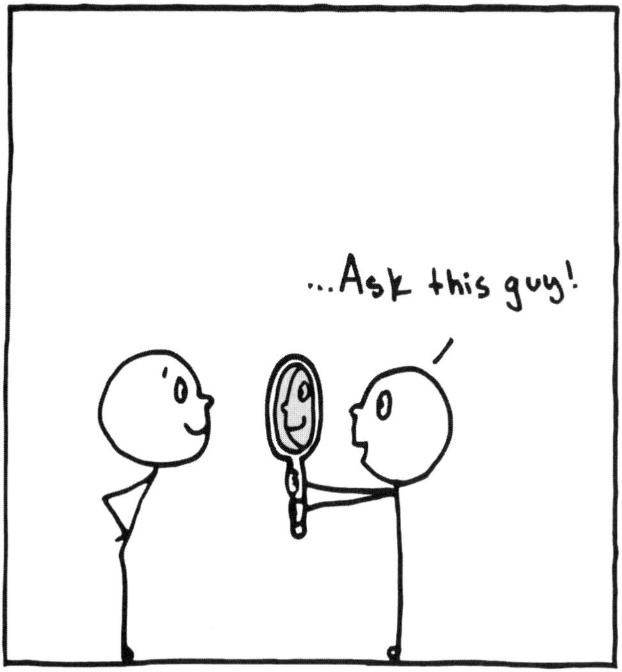
...Ask this guy!

this is fun!
-and hard.
oops!
I got you!
This will need reinforcement.
-and reassurance
Worth it.
Totally.

Building Trust.

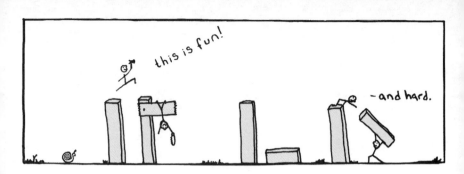

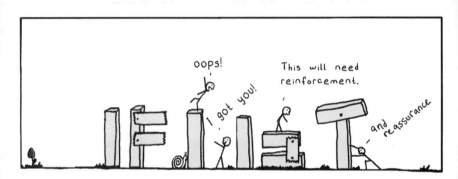

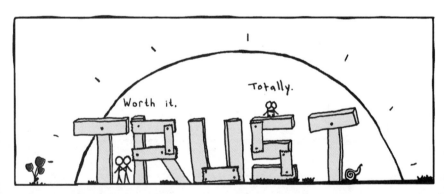

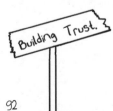

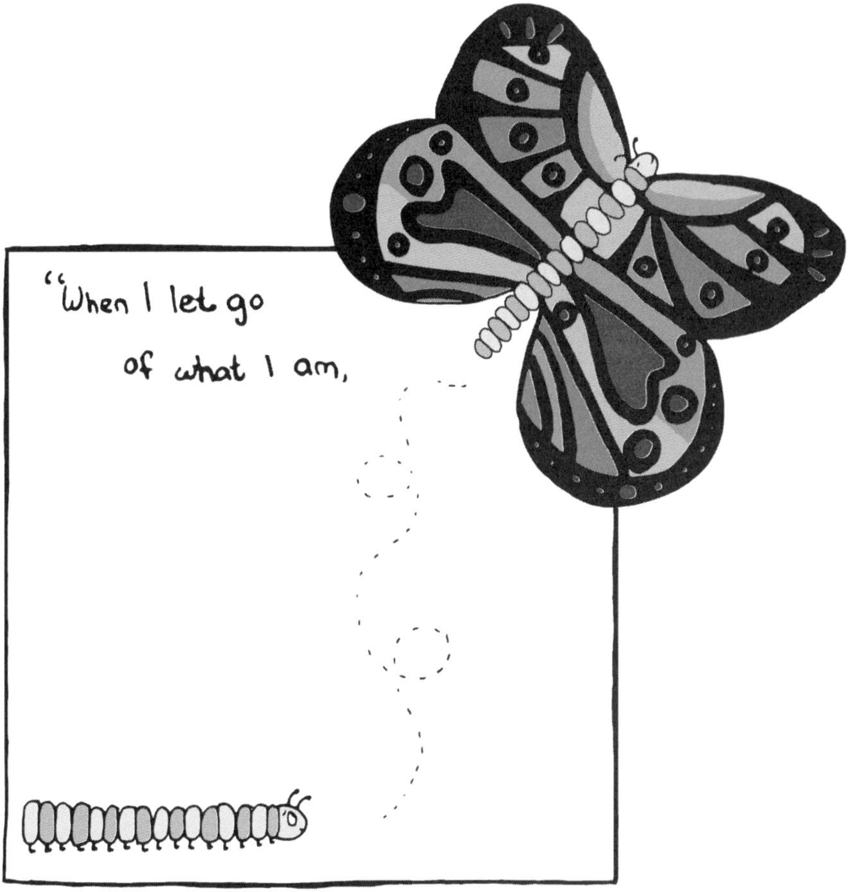
"When I let go
of what I am,

I become what I might be."

-Lao Tzu

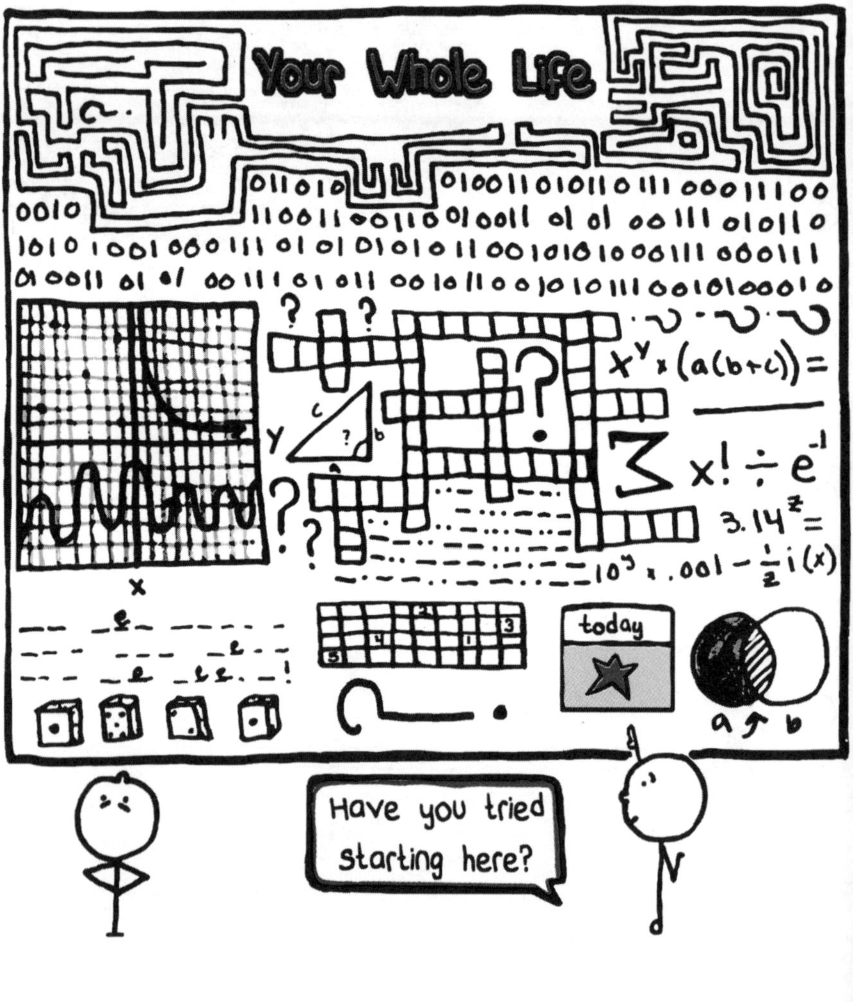
Your Whole Life
today
Have you tried starting here?

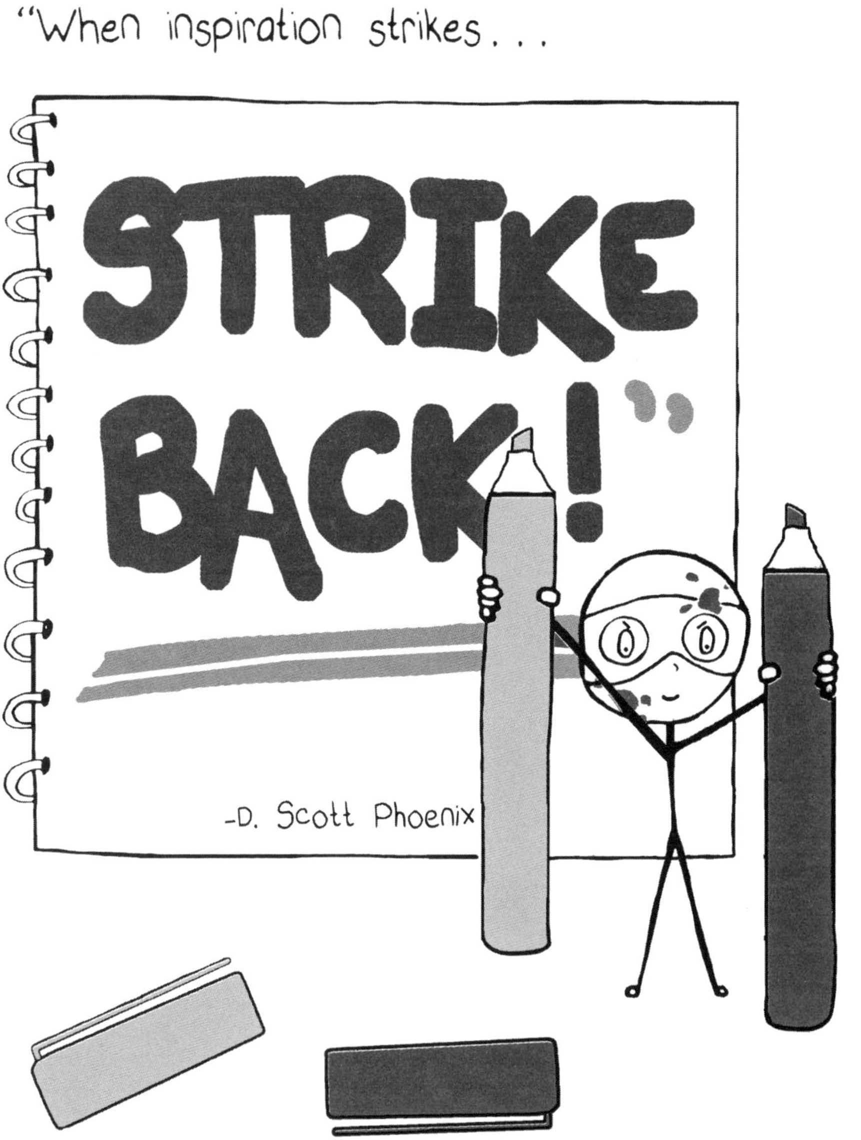
"When inspiration strikes . . .
STRIKE BACK!"
-D. Scott Phoenix

Having a choice isn't freedom...

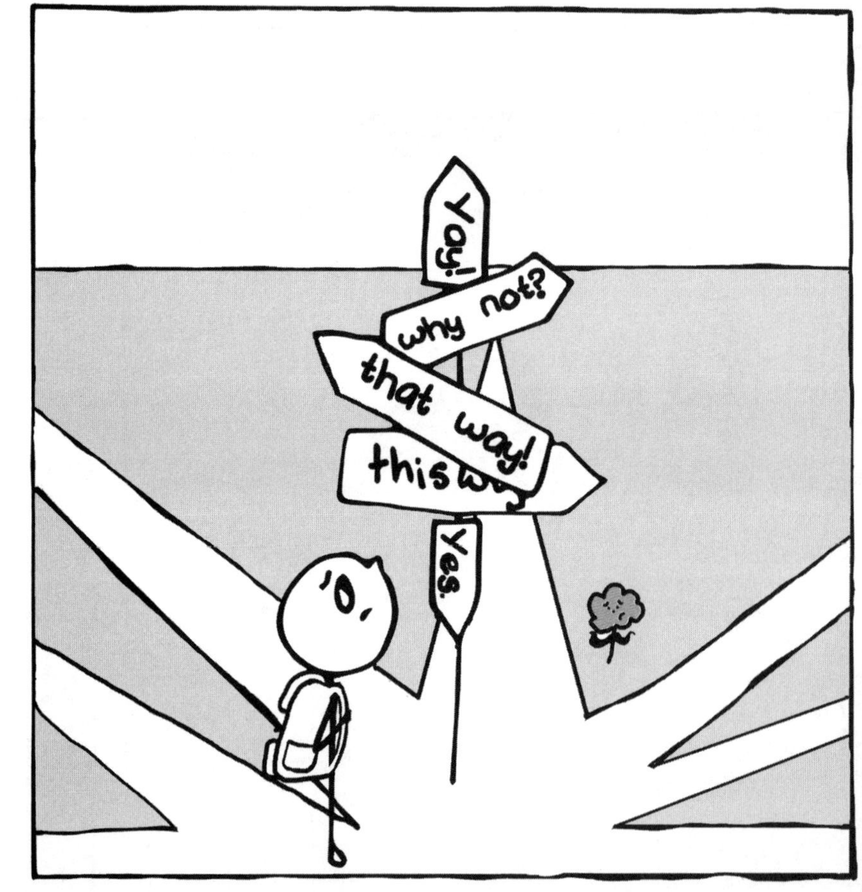

Yay!
why not?
that way!
this way
Yes.

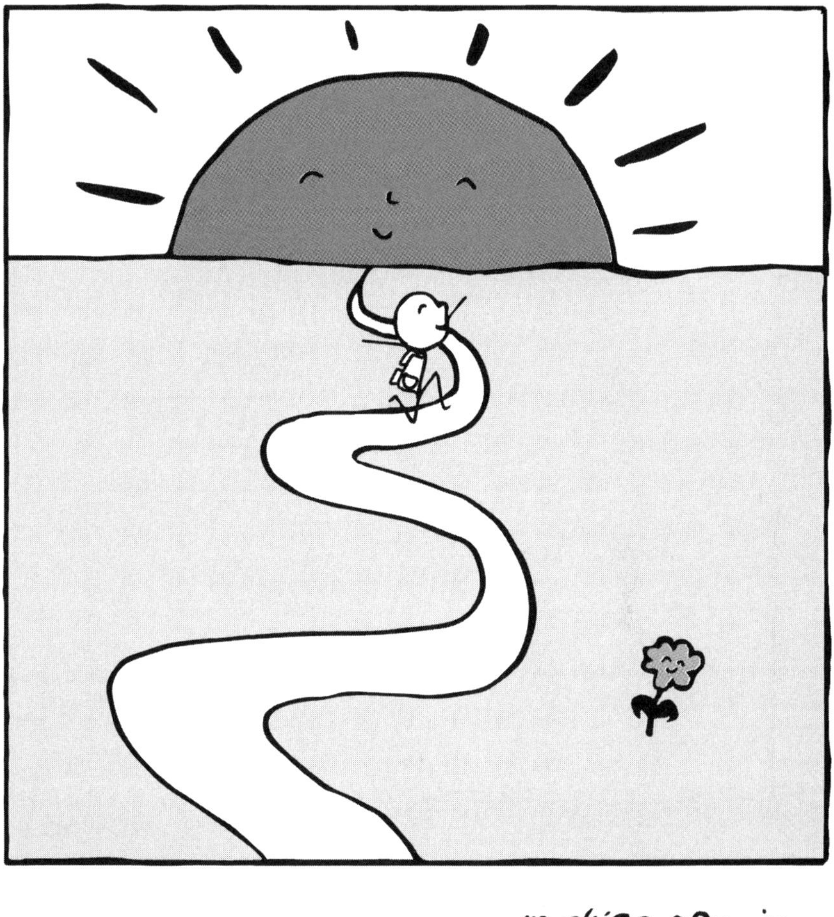

...*making* one is.

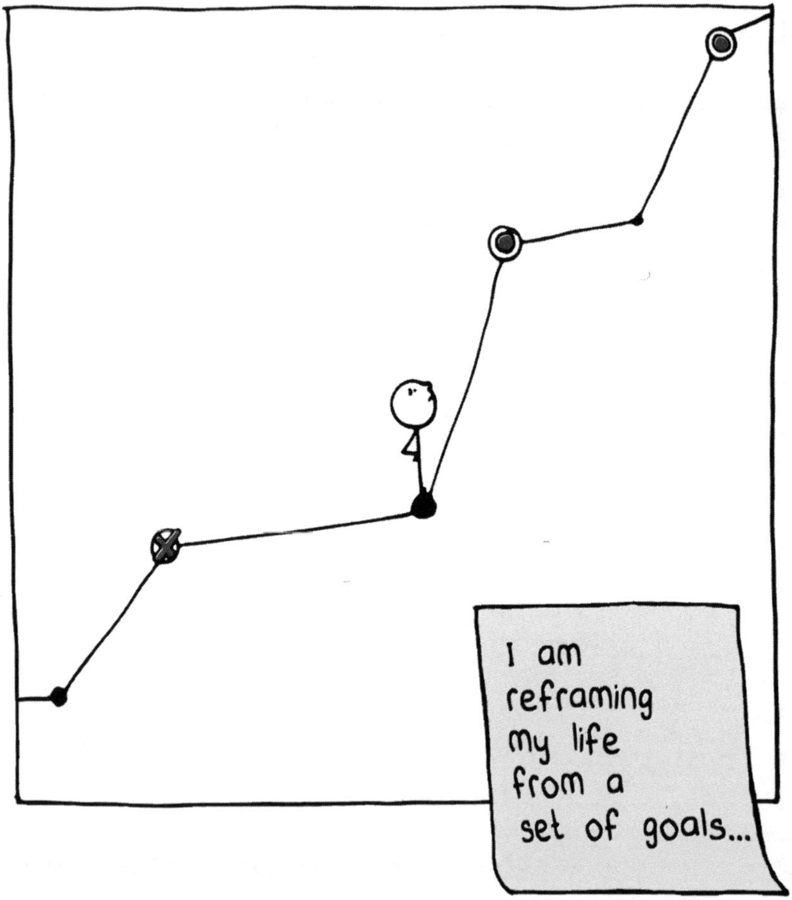
I am
reframing
my life
from a
set of goals...

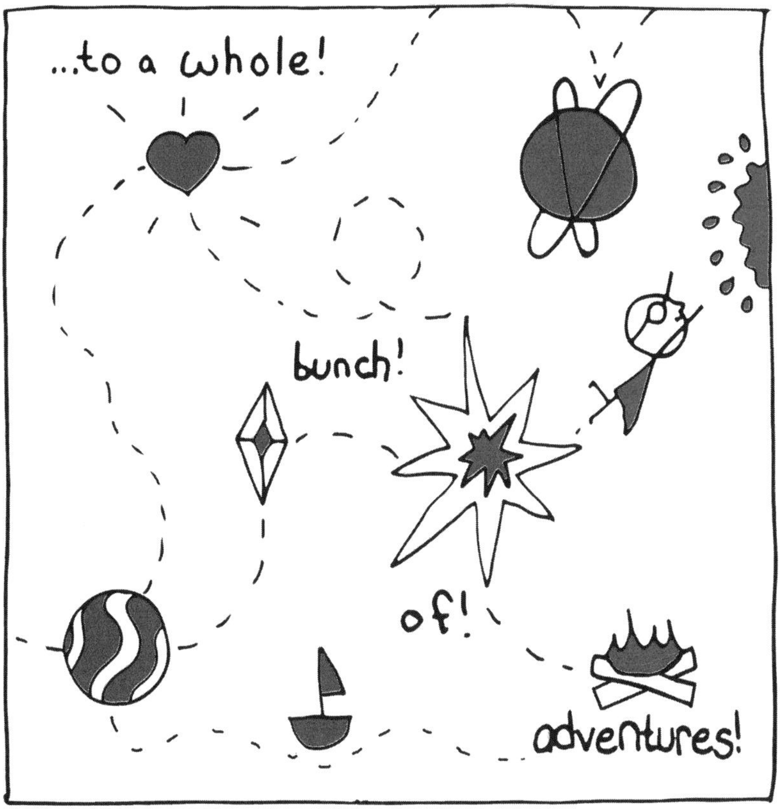
...to a whole!
bunch!
of!
adventures!

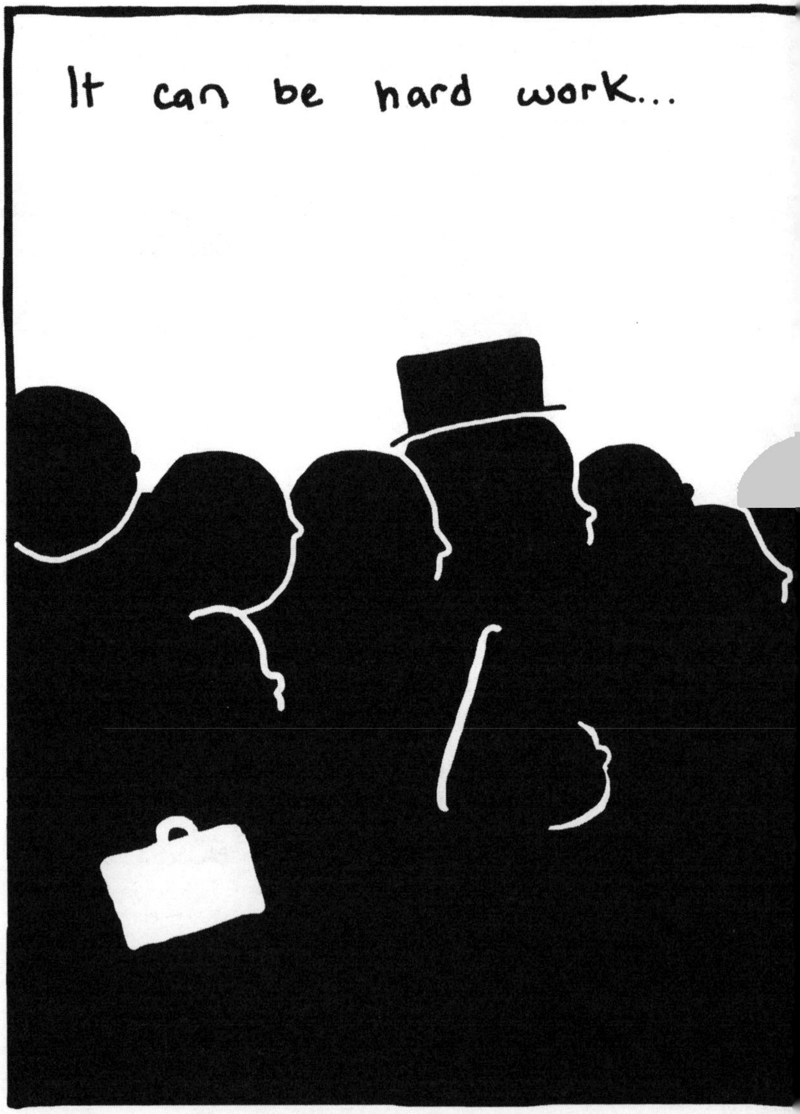
It can be hard work...

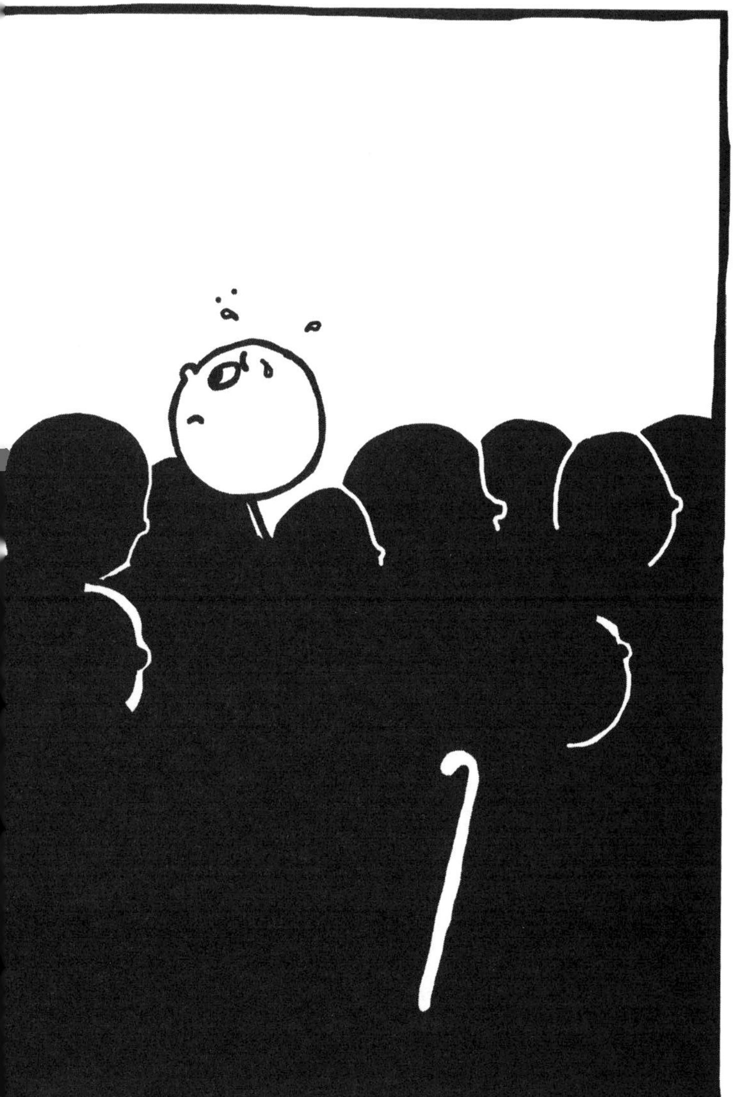

...moving against the crowd.

When you stop LOVING what you're doing...

...stop **DOING** what you're doing.

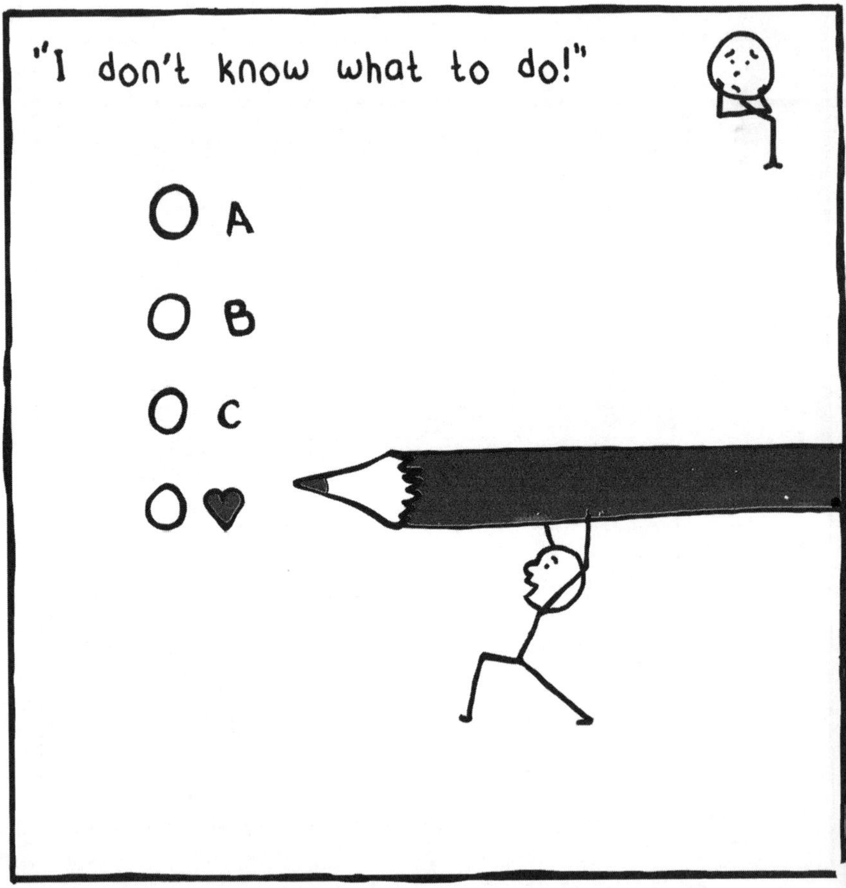
"I don't know what to do!"
A
B
C

"Just keep choosing love." —Justin Rosenstein

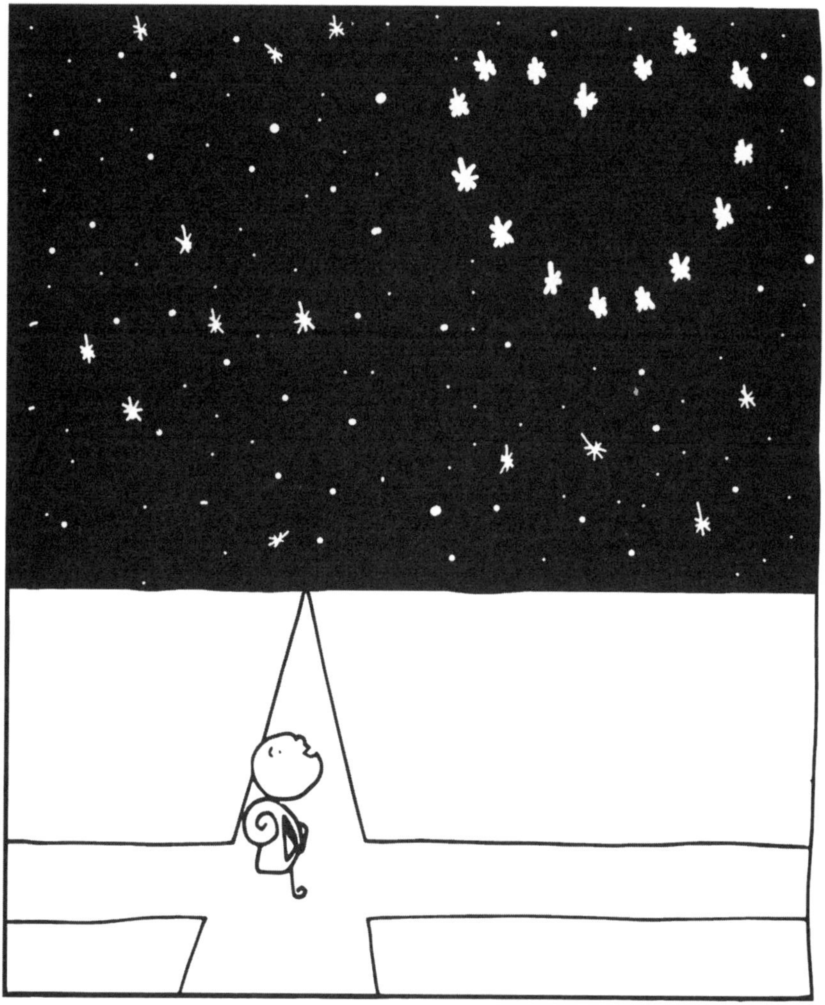

"If ever in doubt, always let kindness be your guide."

—Byron Katie

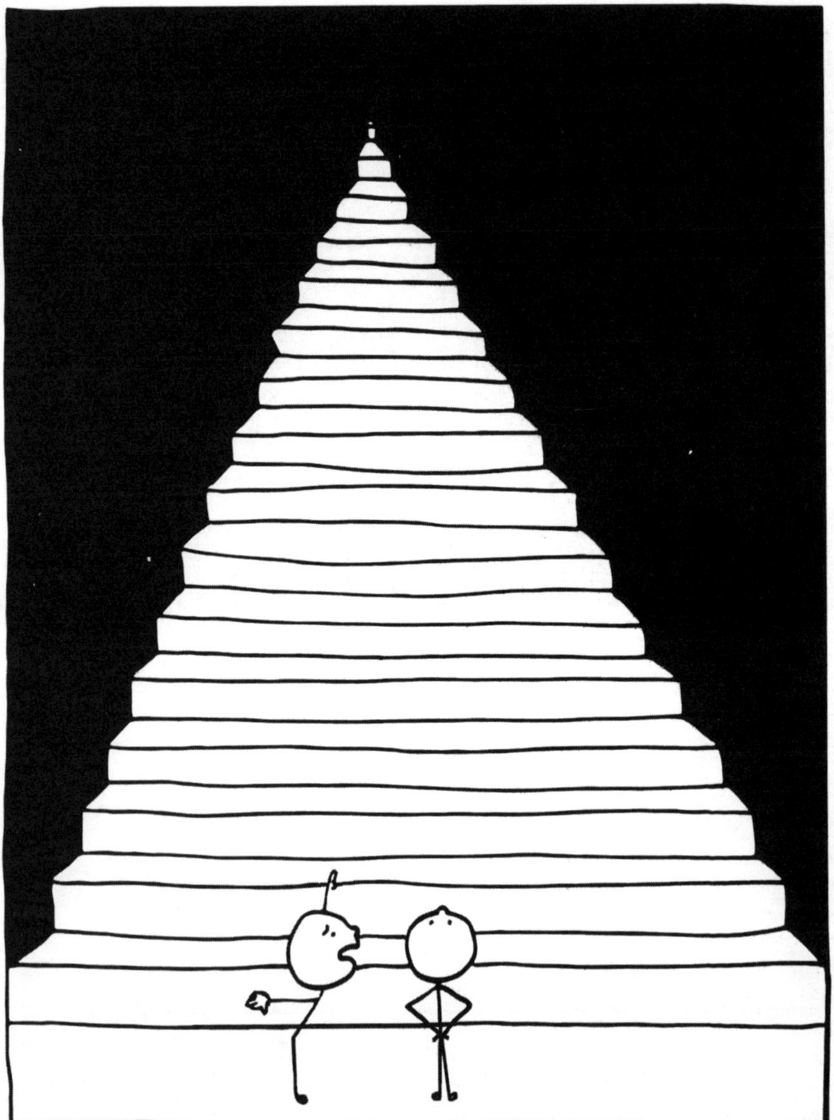

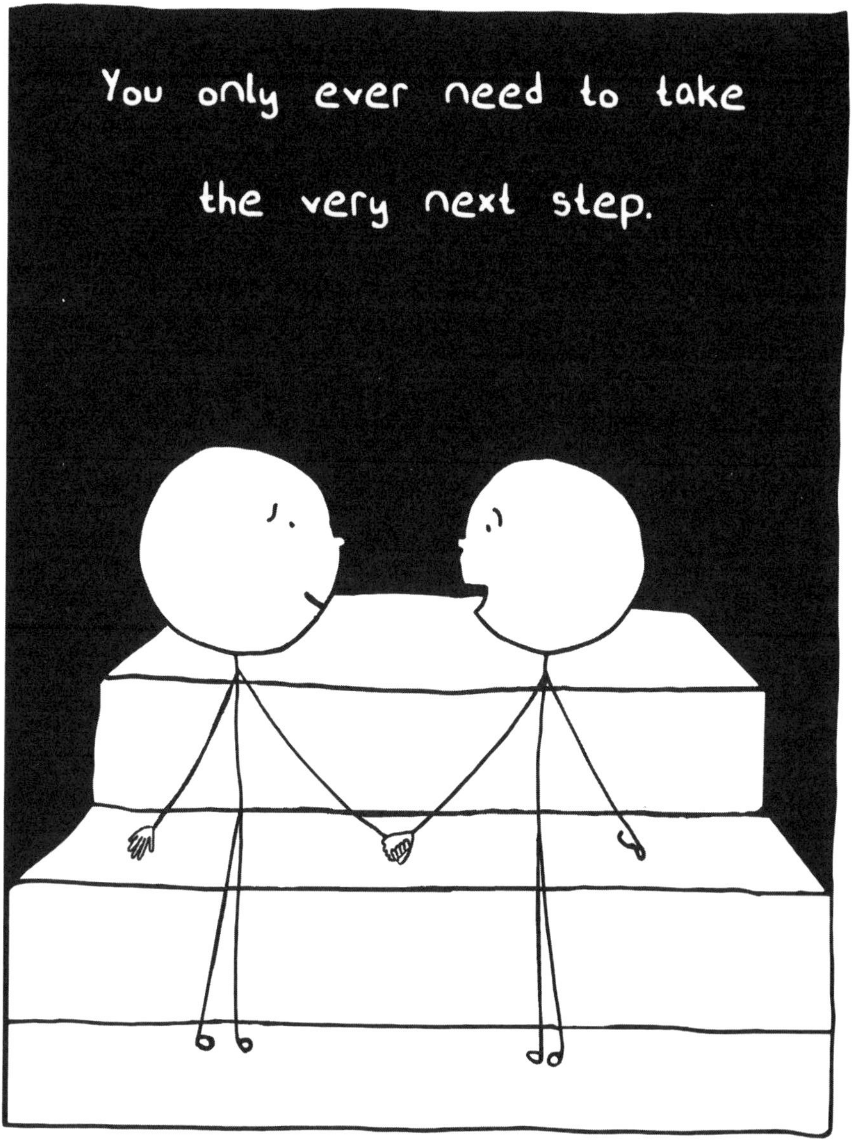
You only ever need to take
the very next step.

"Turn the worst thing that ever happened to you...

...into the best thing."
—Jack Heart

The newest bestseller in self-help:

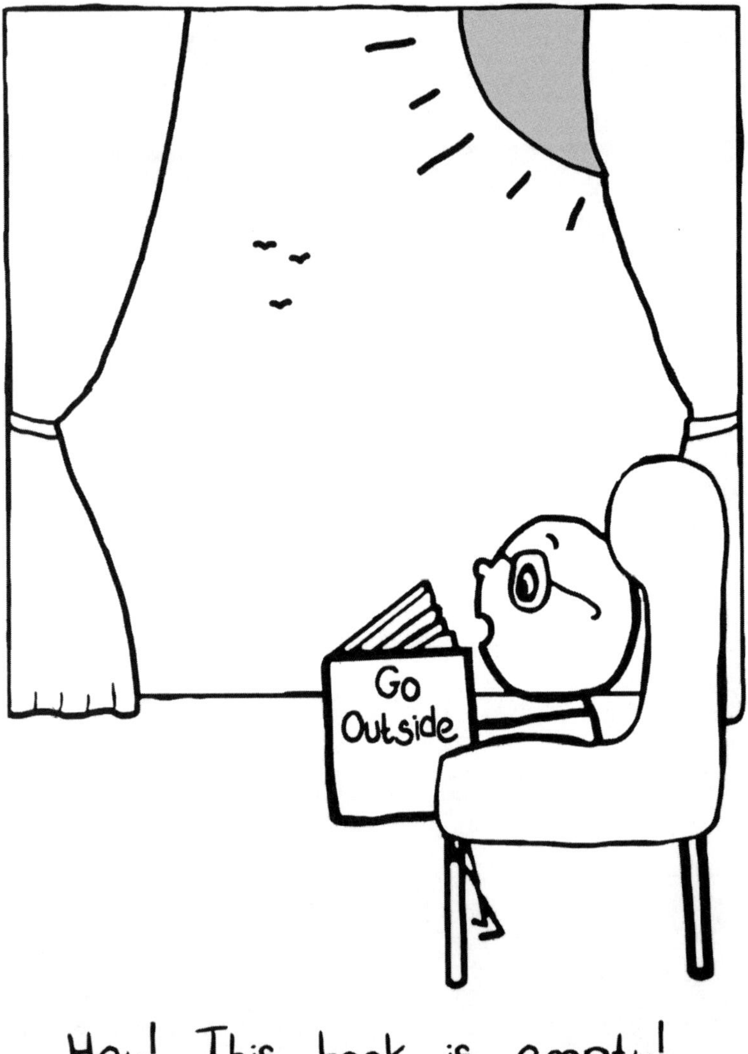
Go
Outside

Hey! This book is empty!

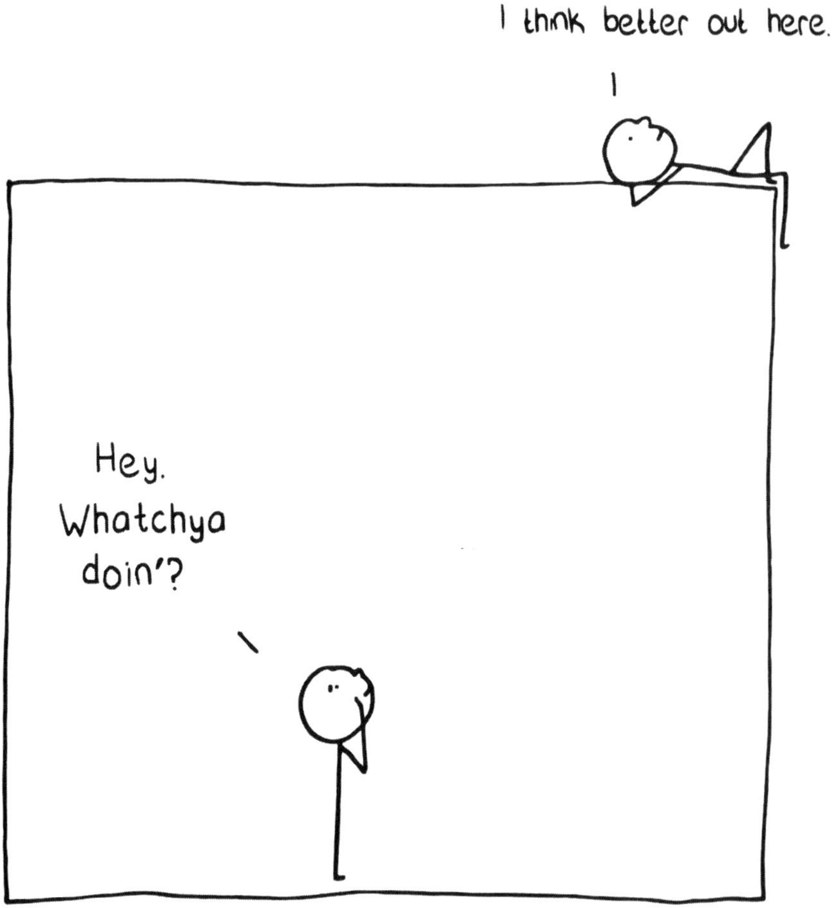
I think better out here.
Hey. Whatchya doin'?

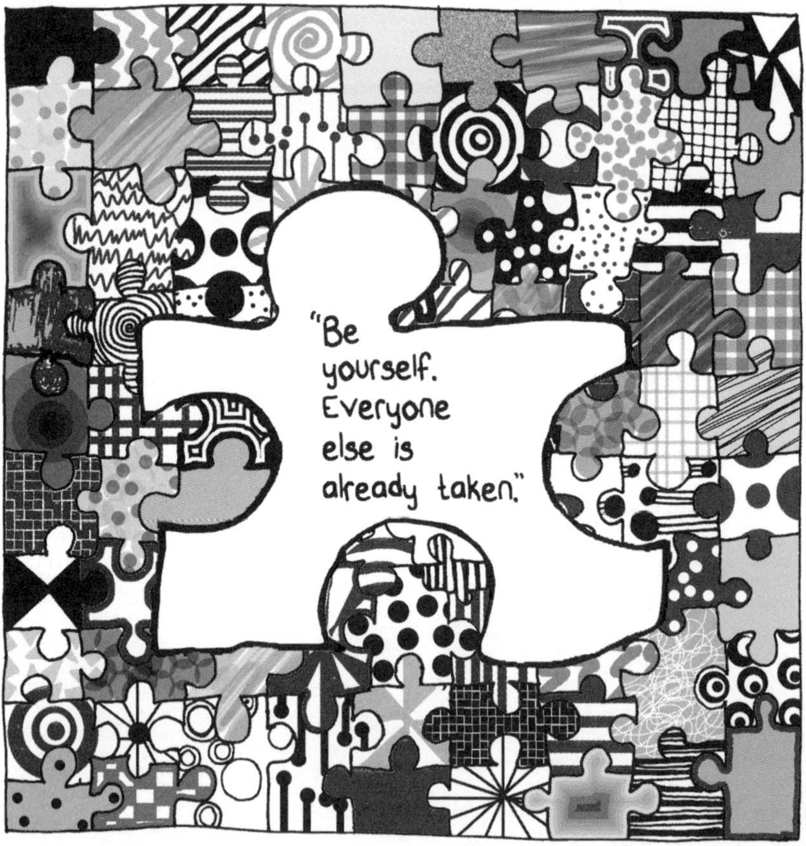
"Be
yourself.
Everyone
else is
already taken."

-Oscar Wilde

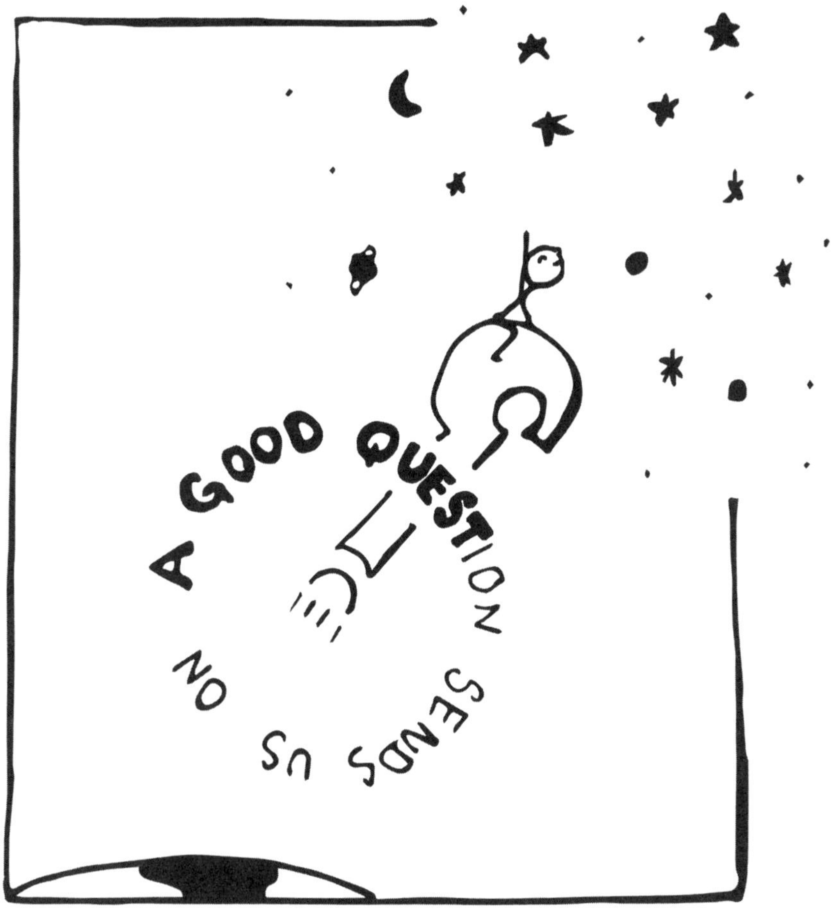
A GOOD QUESTION SENDS US ON

This is *Your* life . . .

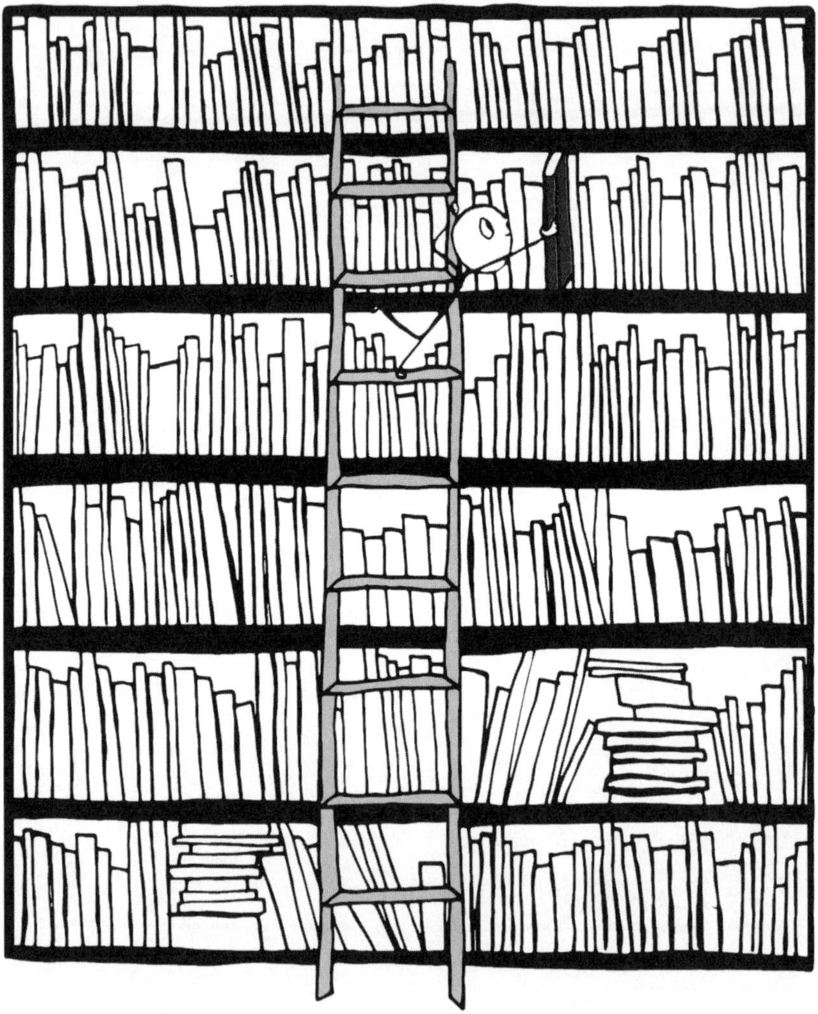

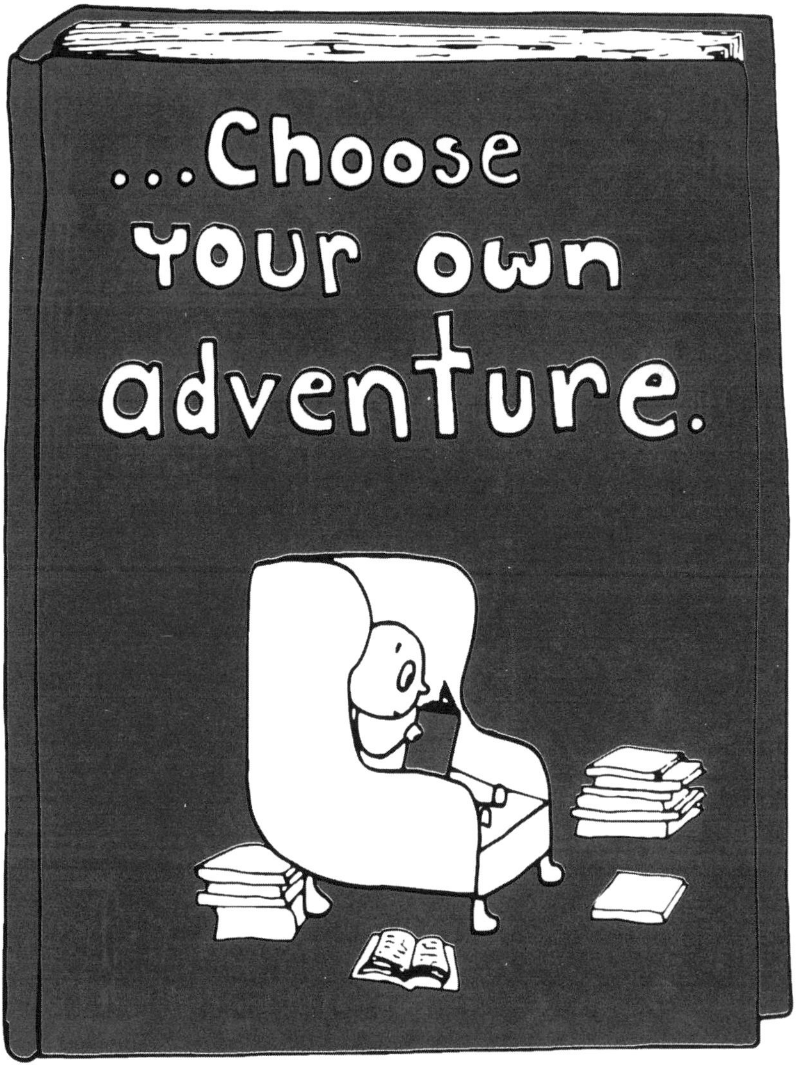
...Choose your own adventure.

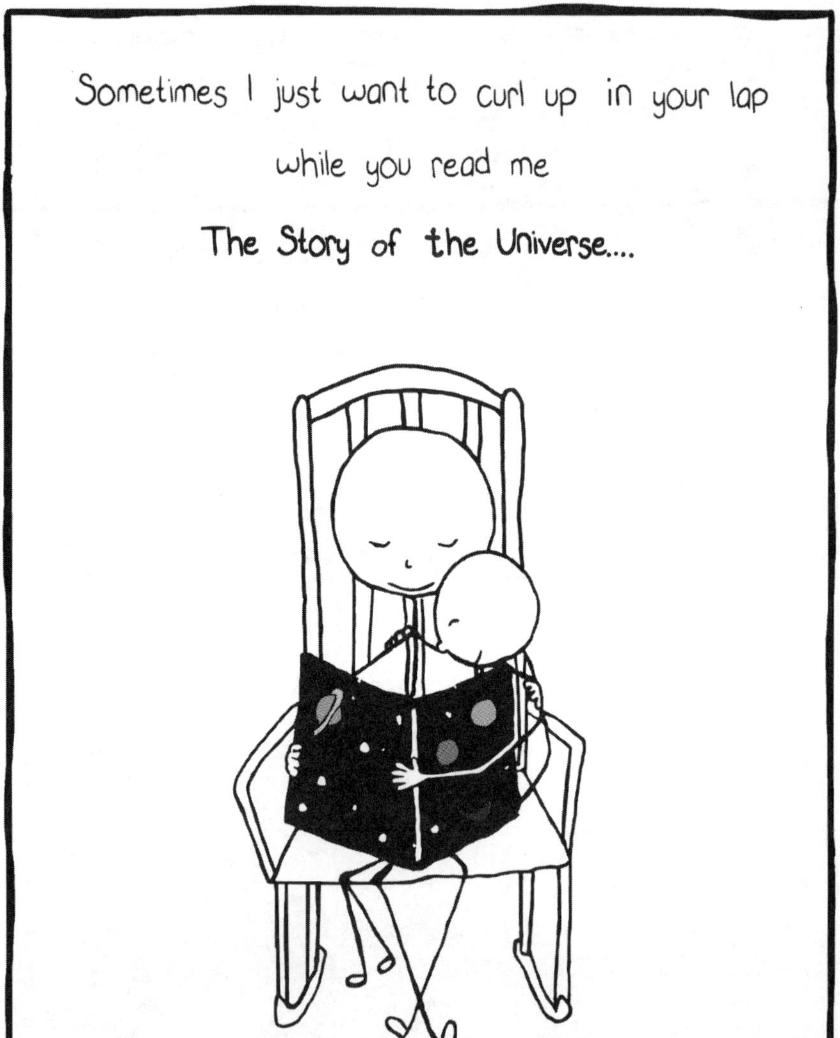
Sometimes I just want to curl up in your lap
while you read me
The Story of the Universe....

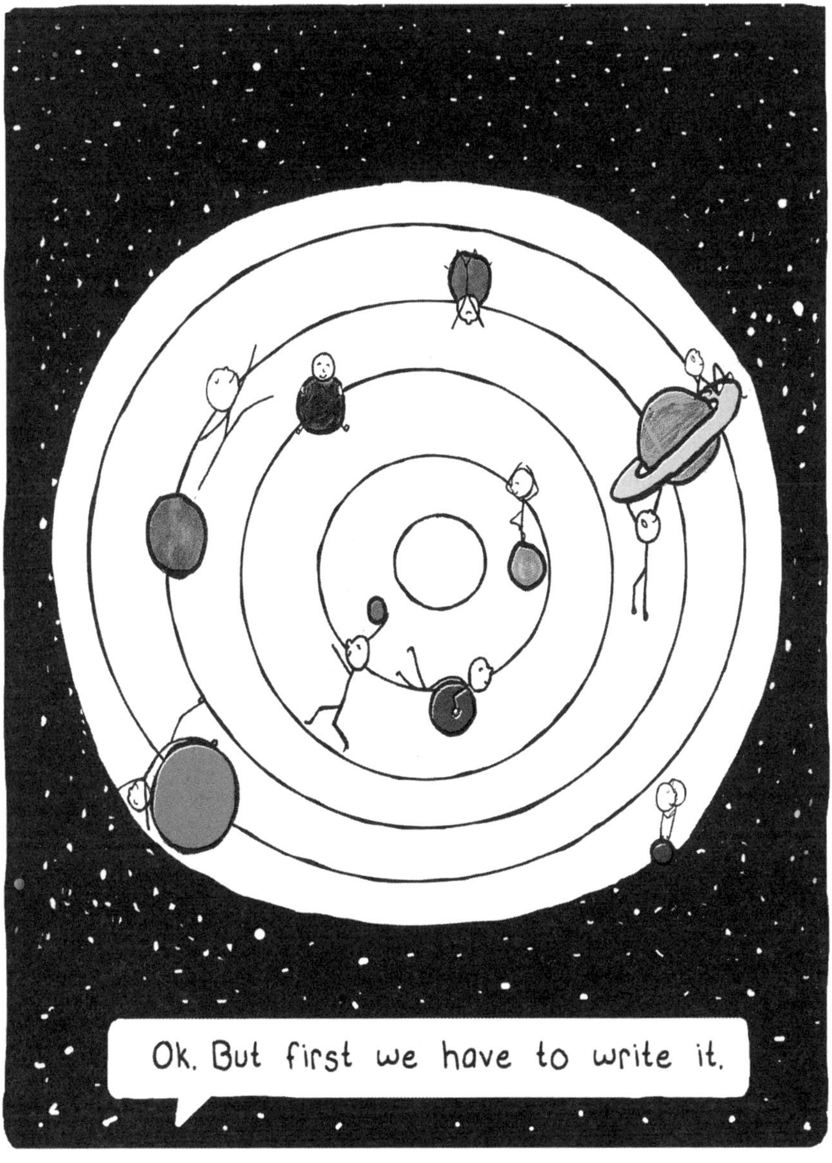
Ok. But first we have to write it.

Five:

Finding the Missing Peace

The Reunion

Beneath all the feeling
Before all the thought
Between the illusions
Of who I am not,

There is a quiet space
A place I can go
Where there's nothing to do
And nothing to know.

I go to remember
The one thing that's true:
To forget whatever
Could keep me from you.

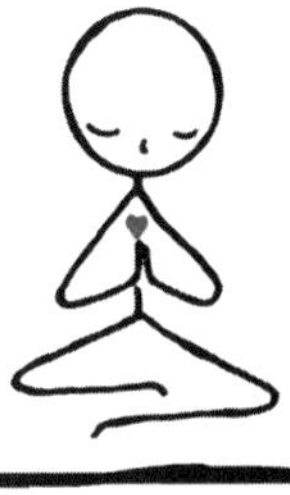

I am finding the antidote to **overwhelm**

not by completing more

or by doing less

but by falling

in

Love

with

Stillness.

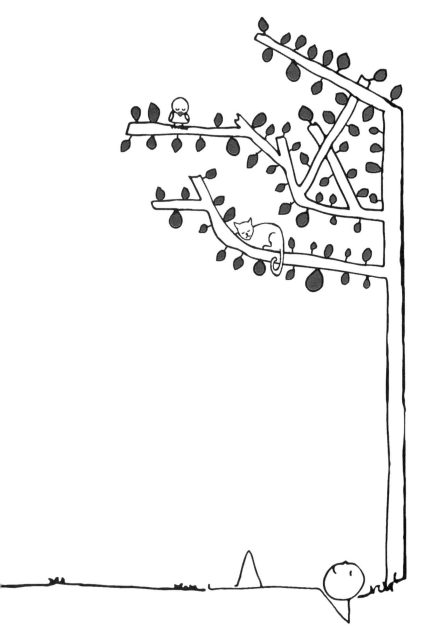

If only mindfulness interrupted life...

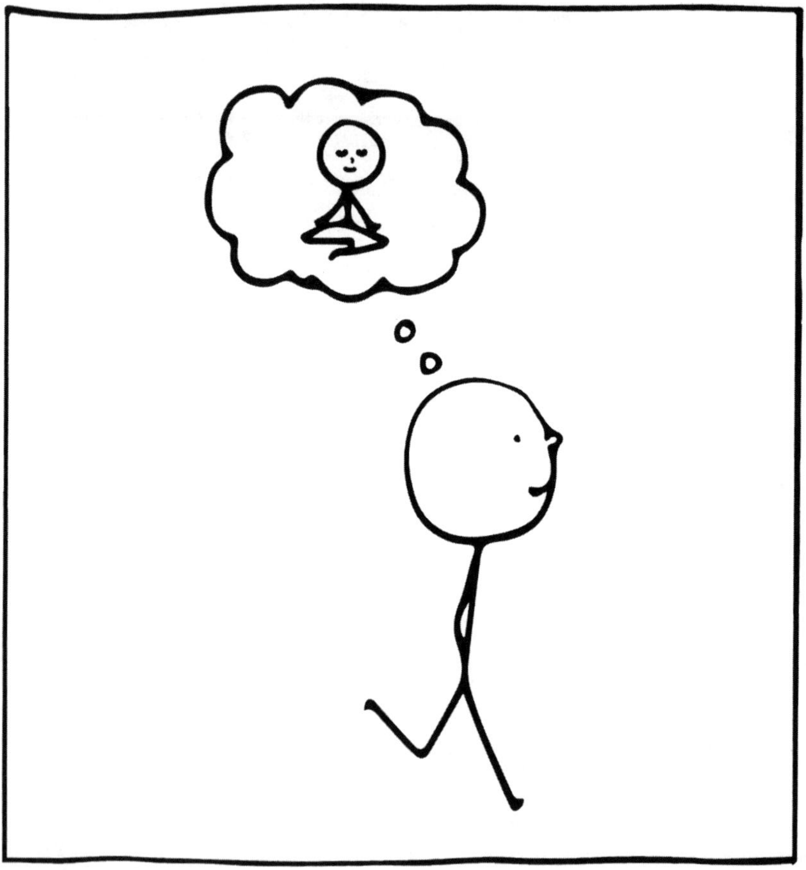

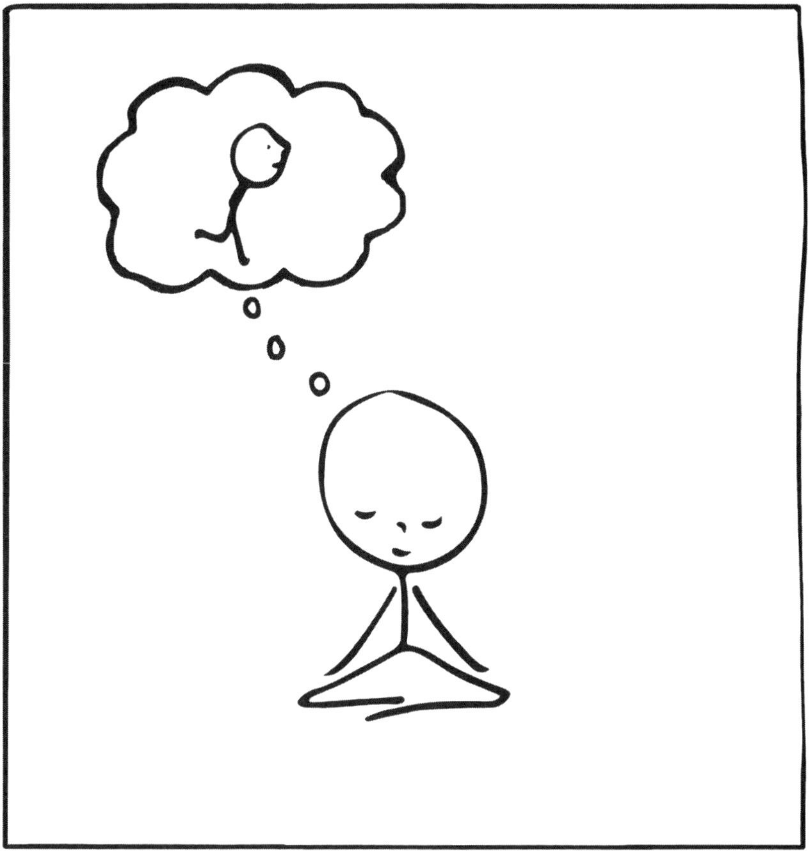

...as much as life interrupts mindfulness.

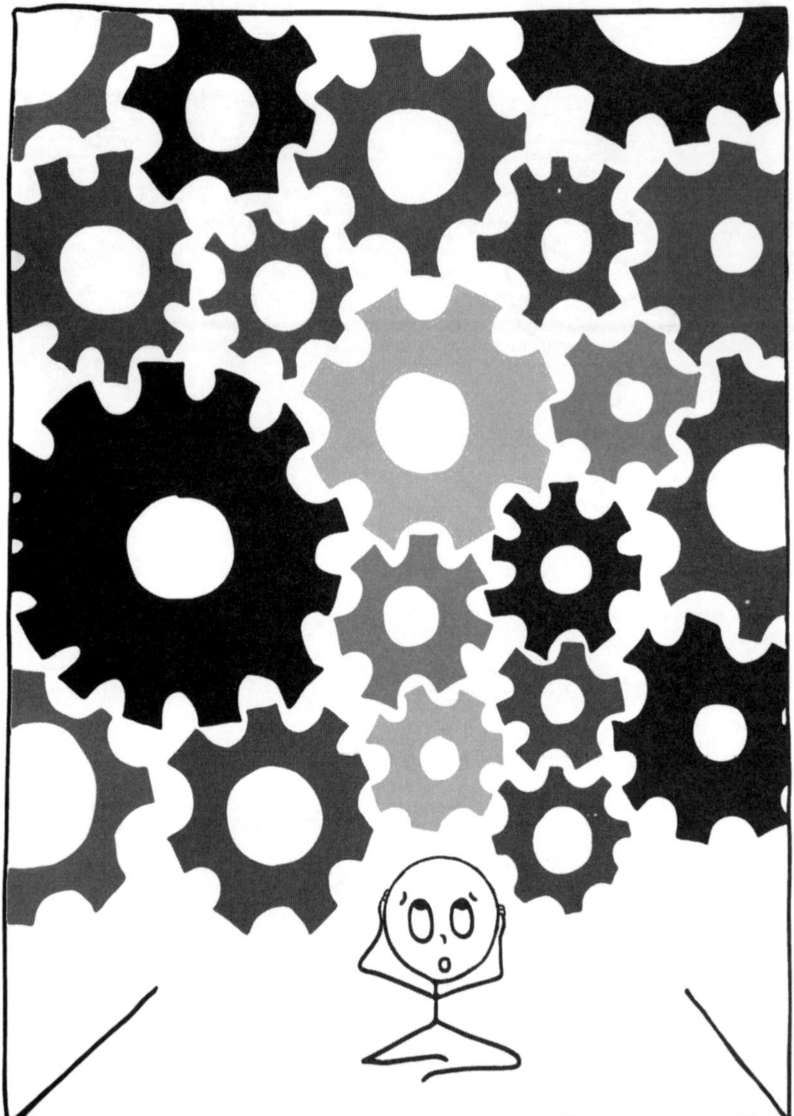

To drown out this noise...

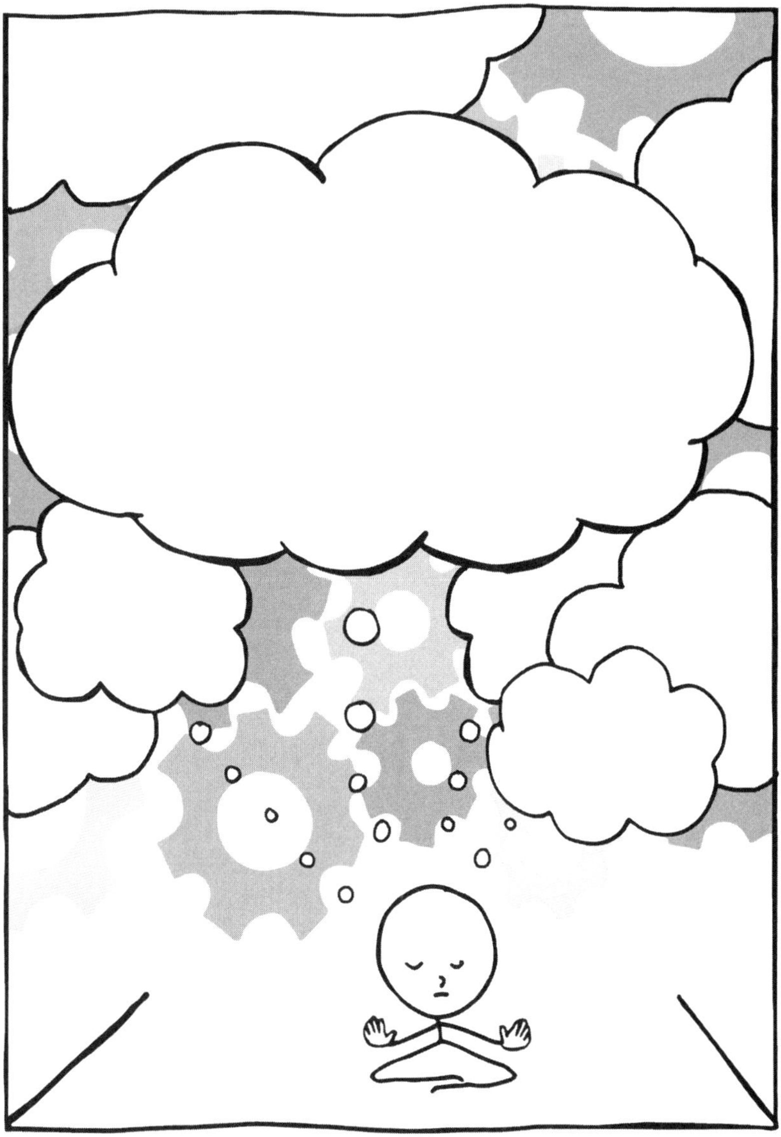

...it takes a whole lot of silence.

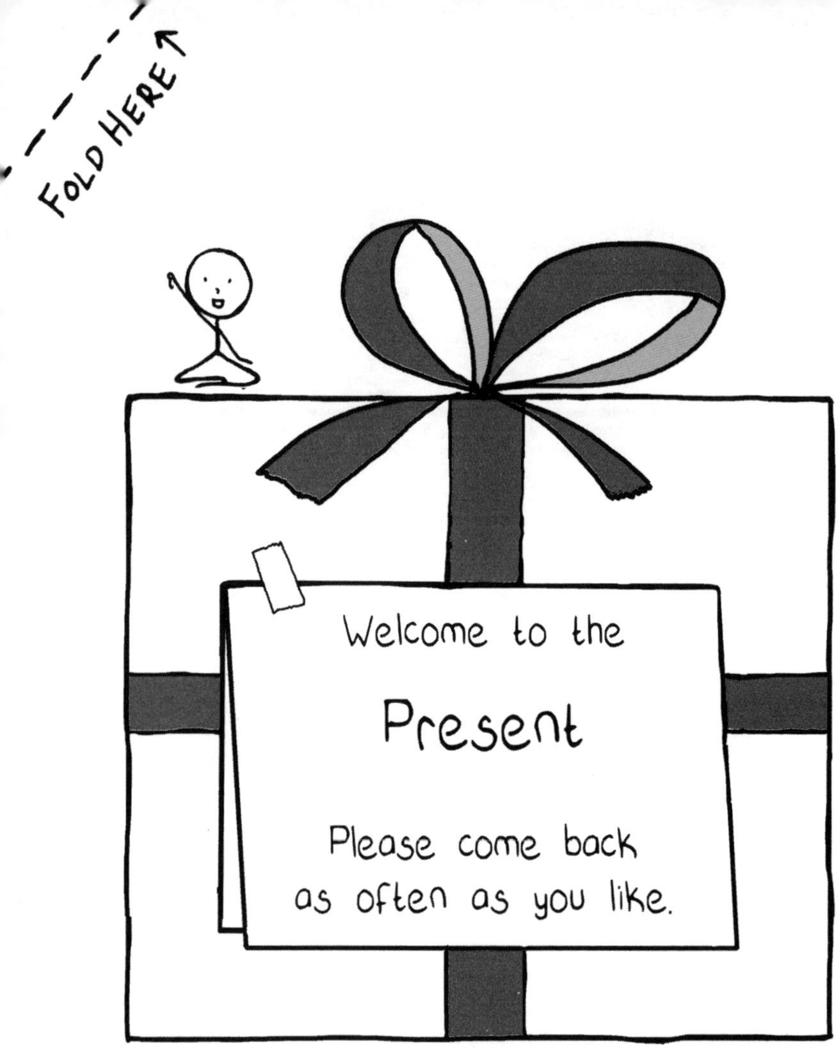
FOLD HERE
Welcome to the
Present
Please come back
as often as you like.

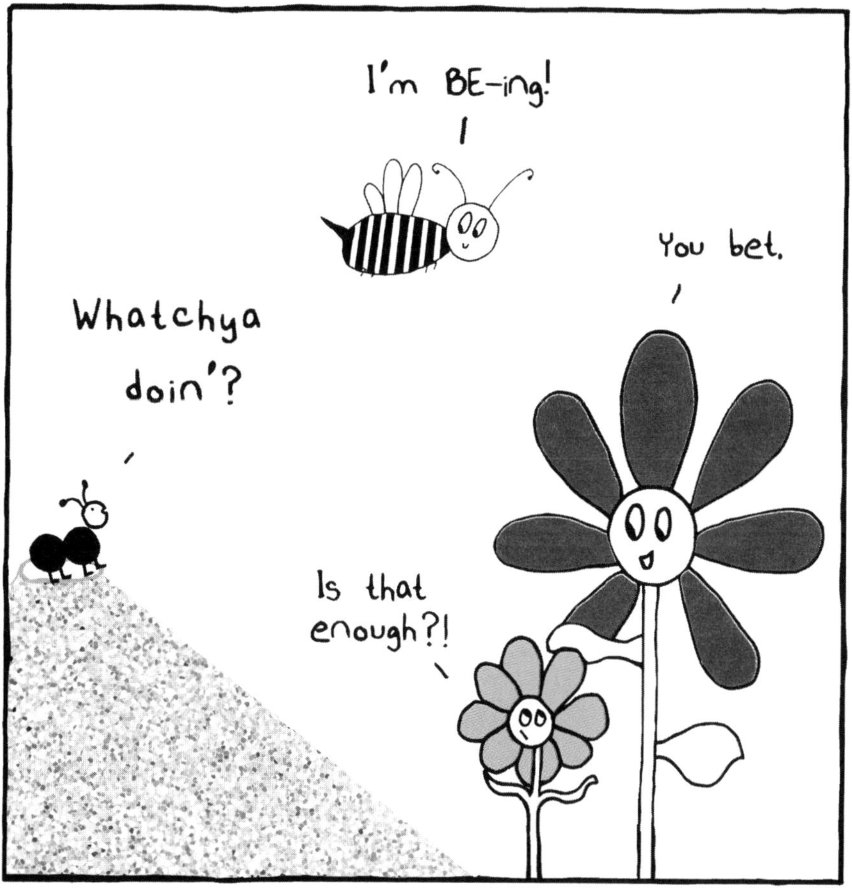
I'm BE-ing!
Whatchya doin'?
You bet.
Is that enough?!

Meditation:

Staying in one place long enough
for YOU to know where to find YOU.

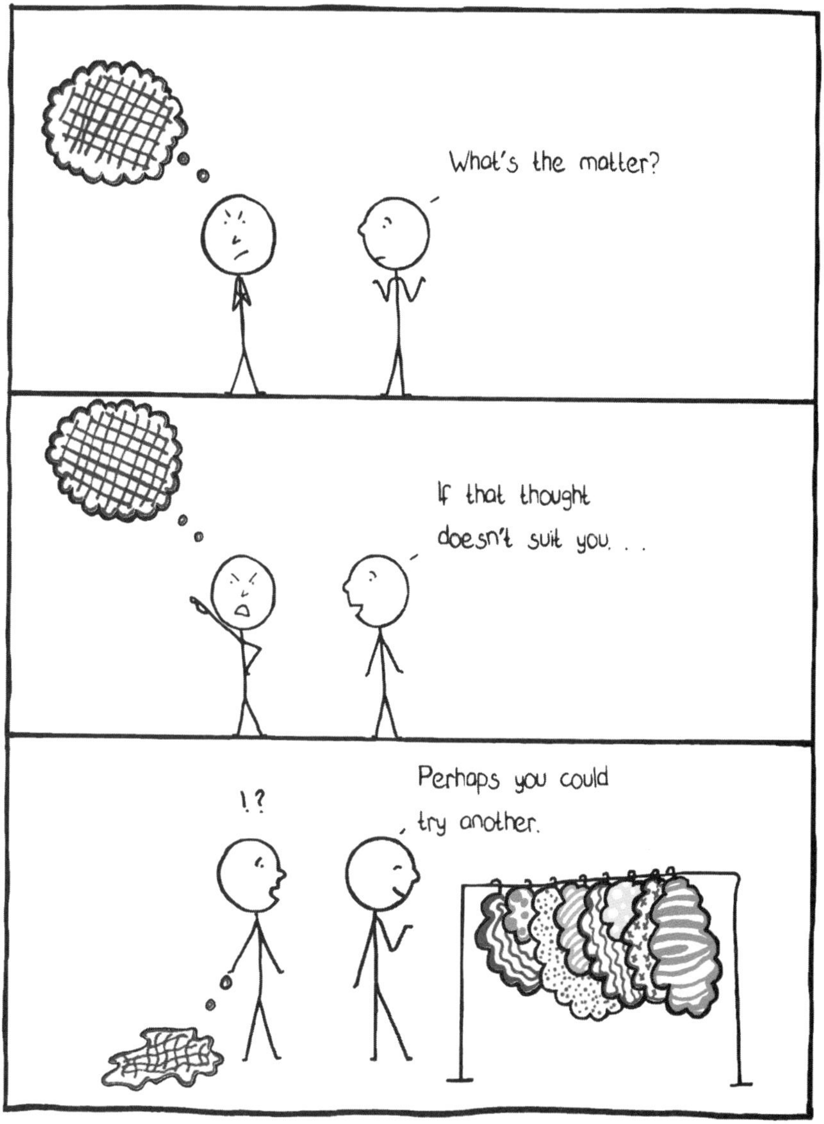
What's the matter?
If that thought doesn't suit you. . .
!?
Perhaps you could try another.

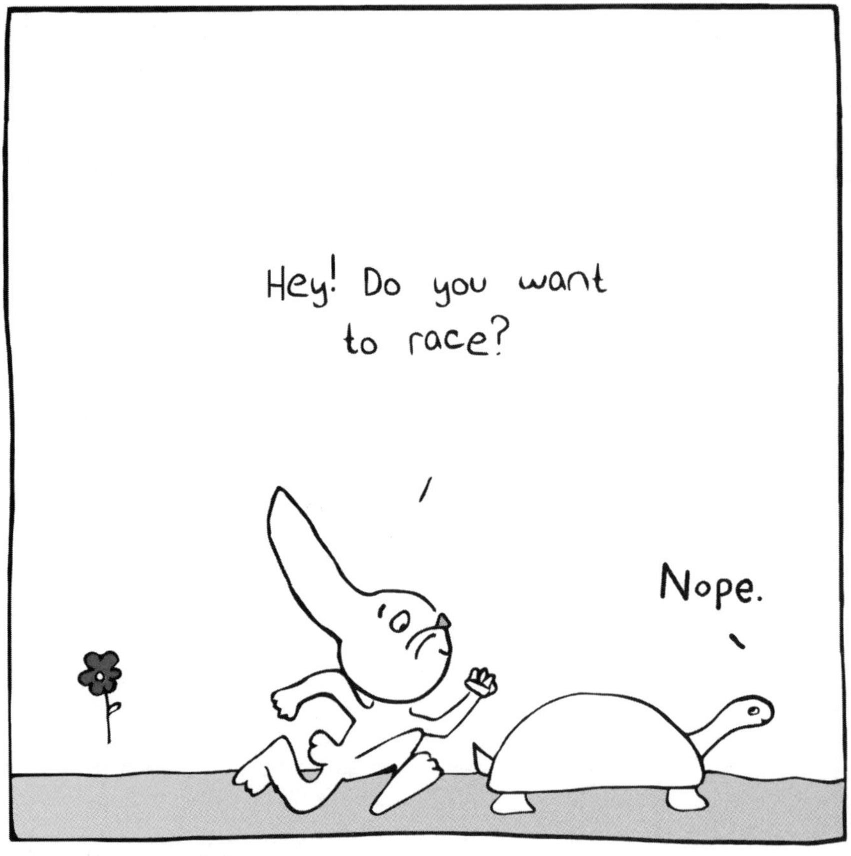
Hey! Do you want to race?
Nope.

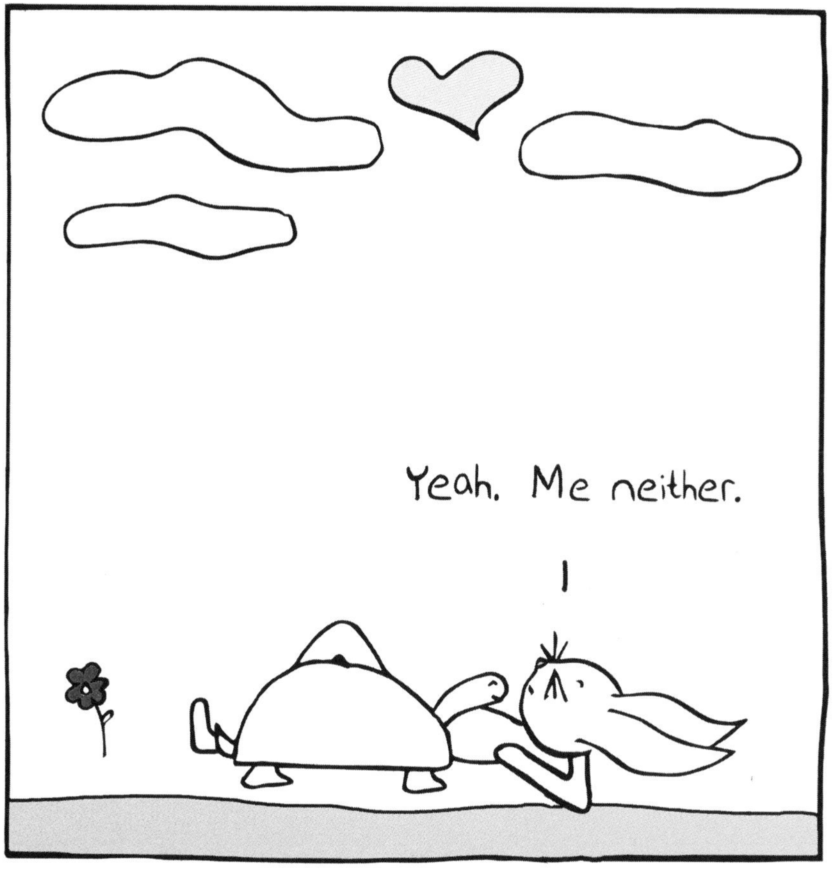
Yeah. Me neither.

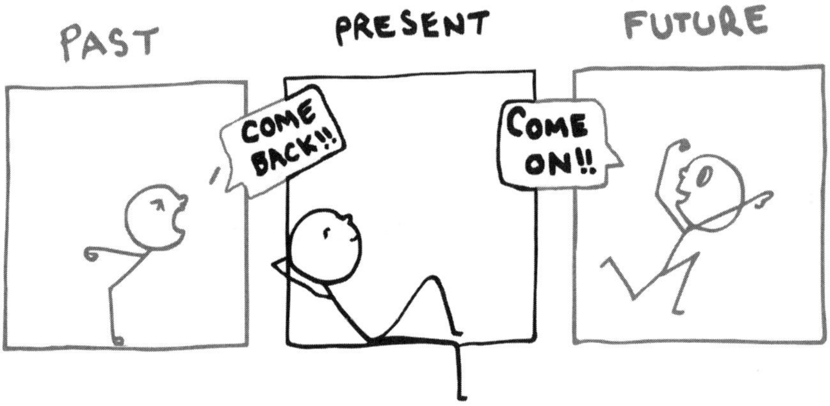
PAST
PRESENT
FUTURE
COME BACK!!
COME ON!!

No, thanks. I'm good here.

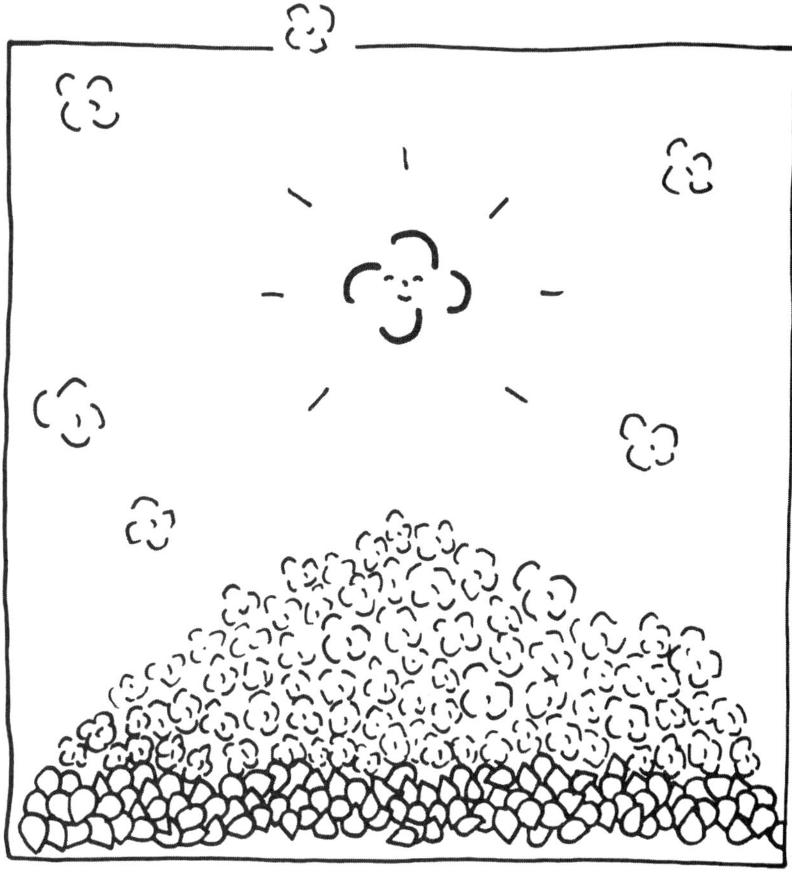

We each pop in our own time.

Watching my M.I.N.D.*

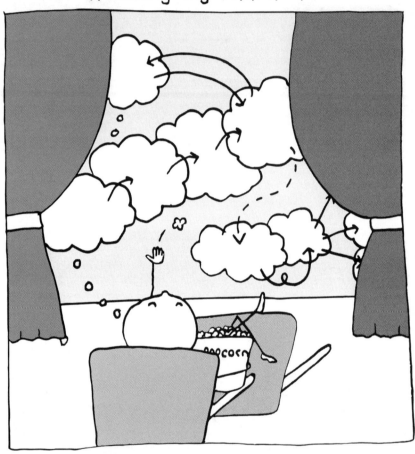

*Mostly Inaccurate Neuro-Drama

How about an

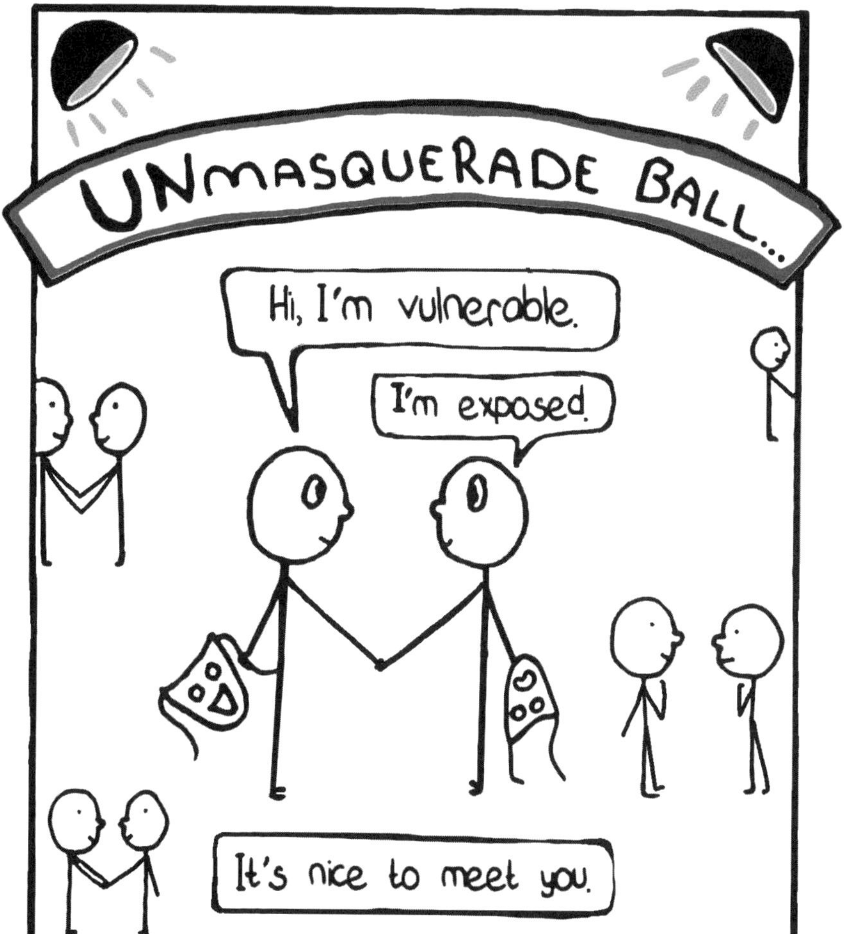
UNMASQUERADE BALL...
Hi, I'm vulnerable.
I'm exposed.
It's nice to meet you.

...Where all the masks come off.

When I get caught up in how much there is to do...

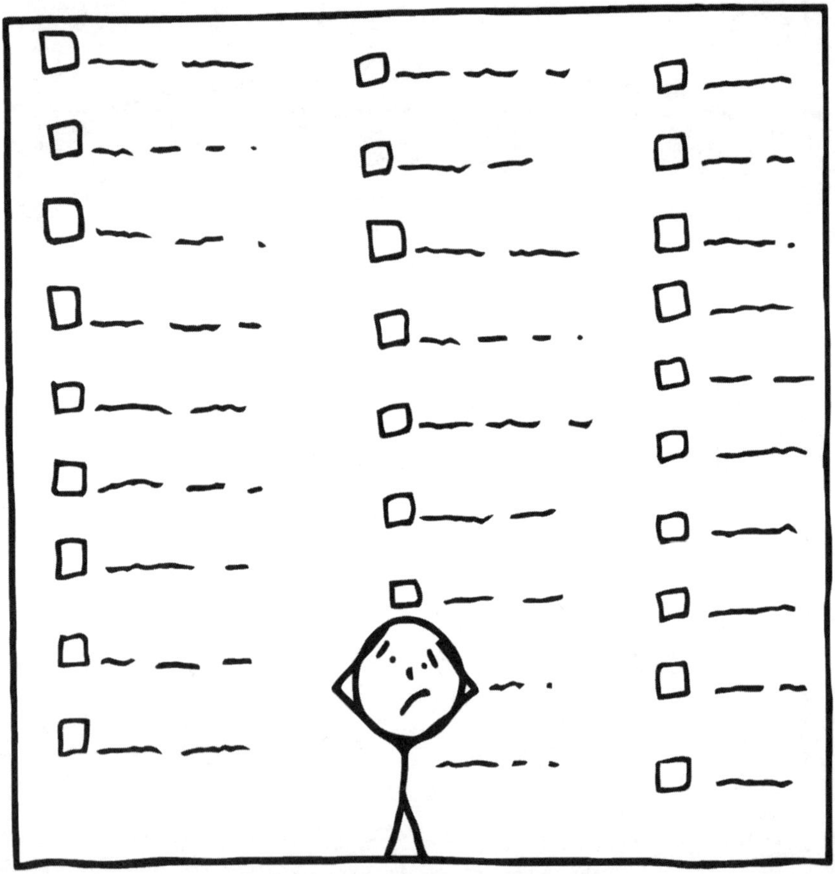

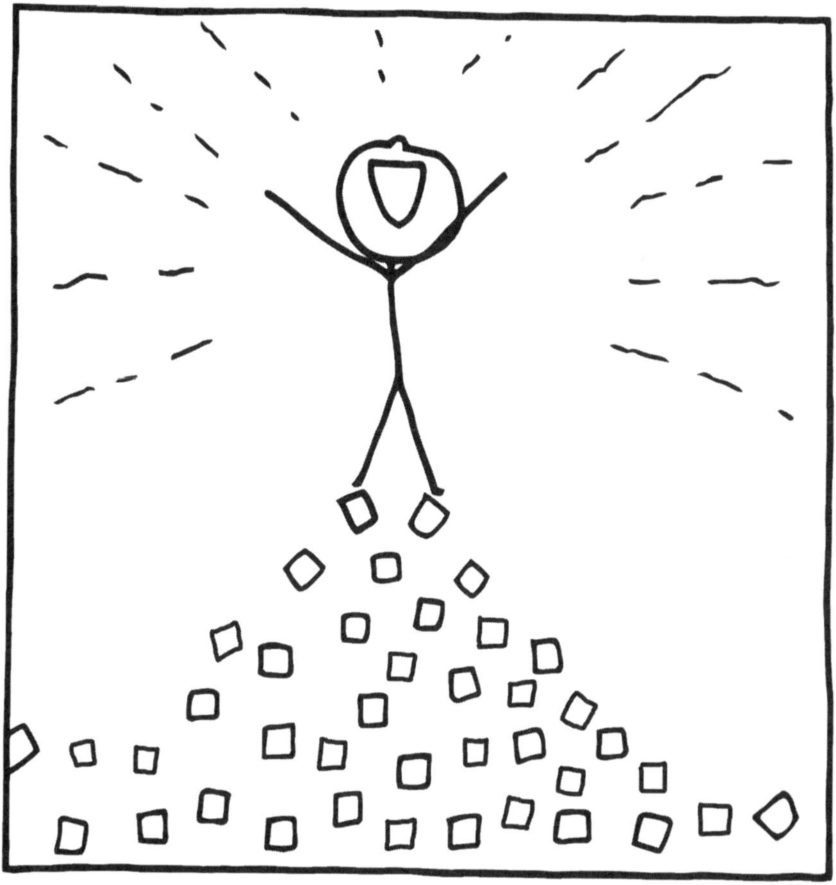

...I like to remember how much there is to be.

Thank you...

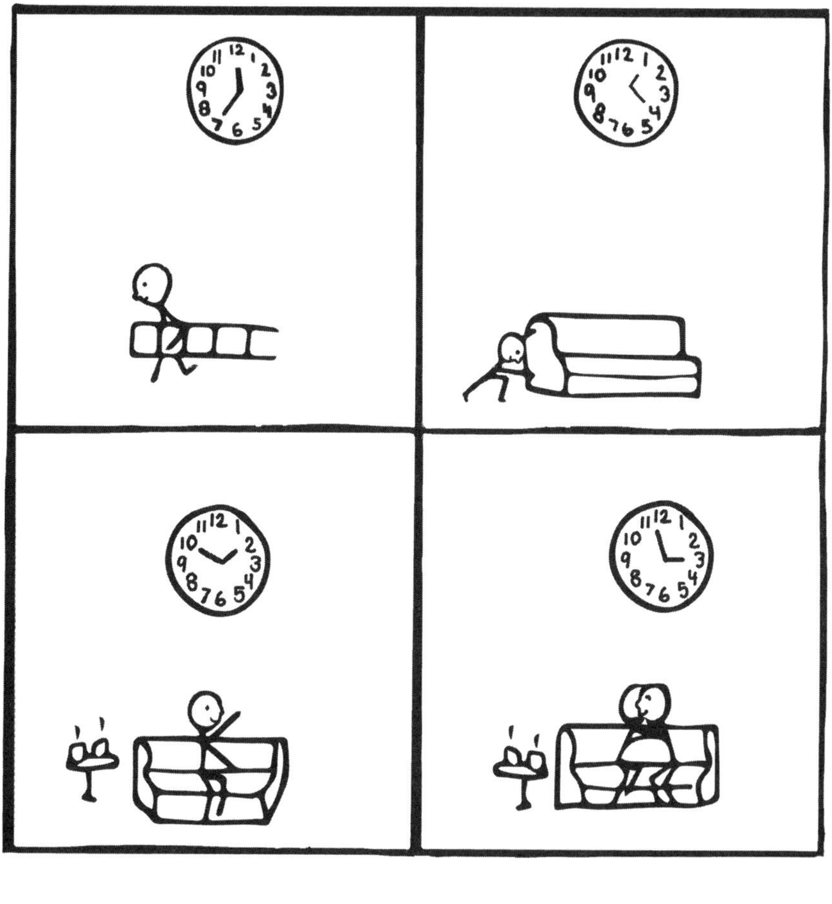

...for making the time.

Rich.

Richer.

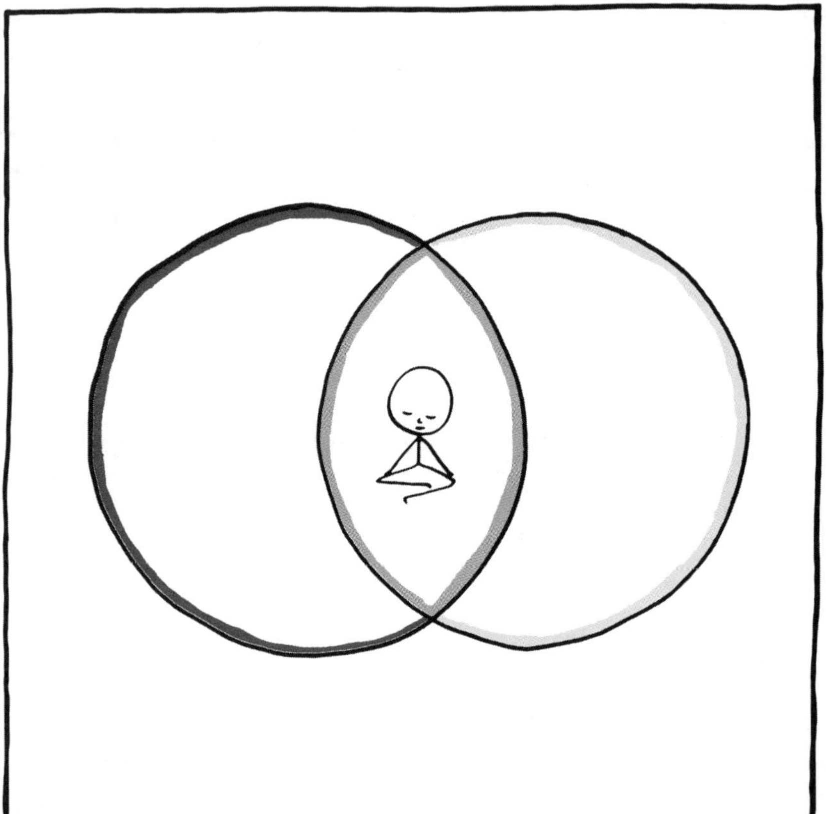

Zen Diagram

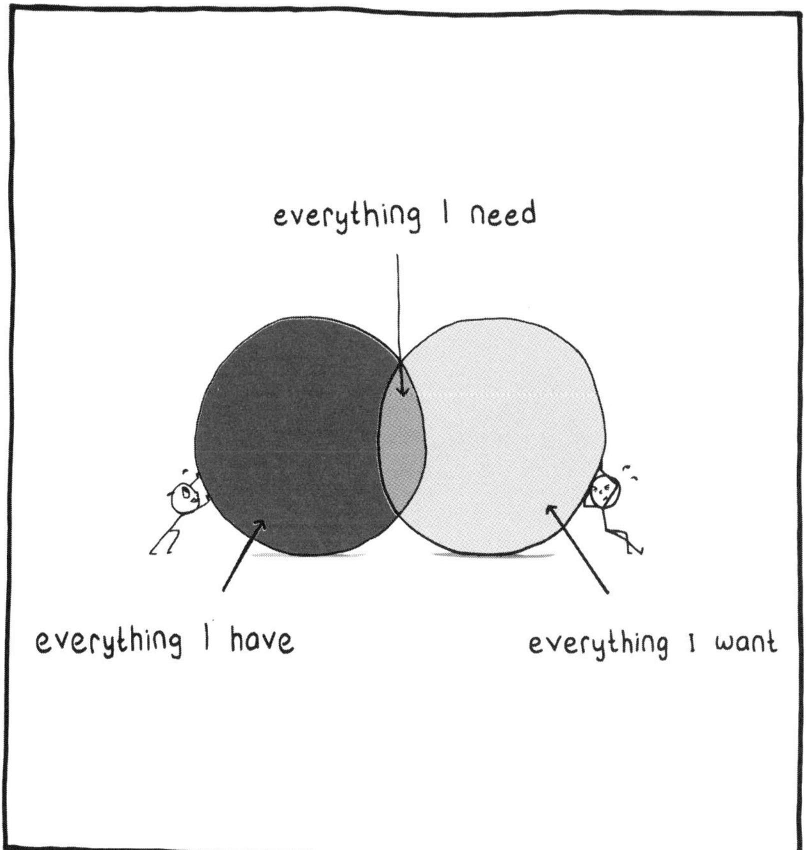
everything I need
everything I have
everything I want

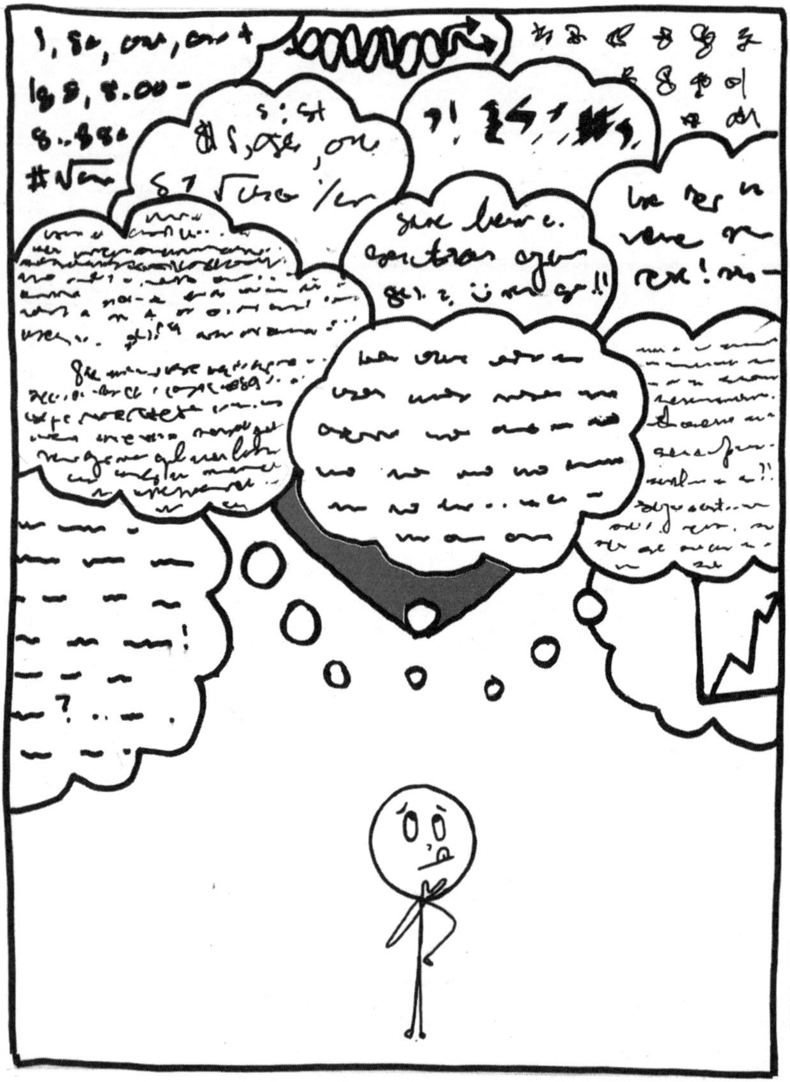

Sometimes it's less about learning...

...and more about unlearning.

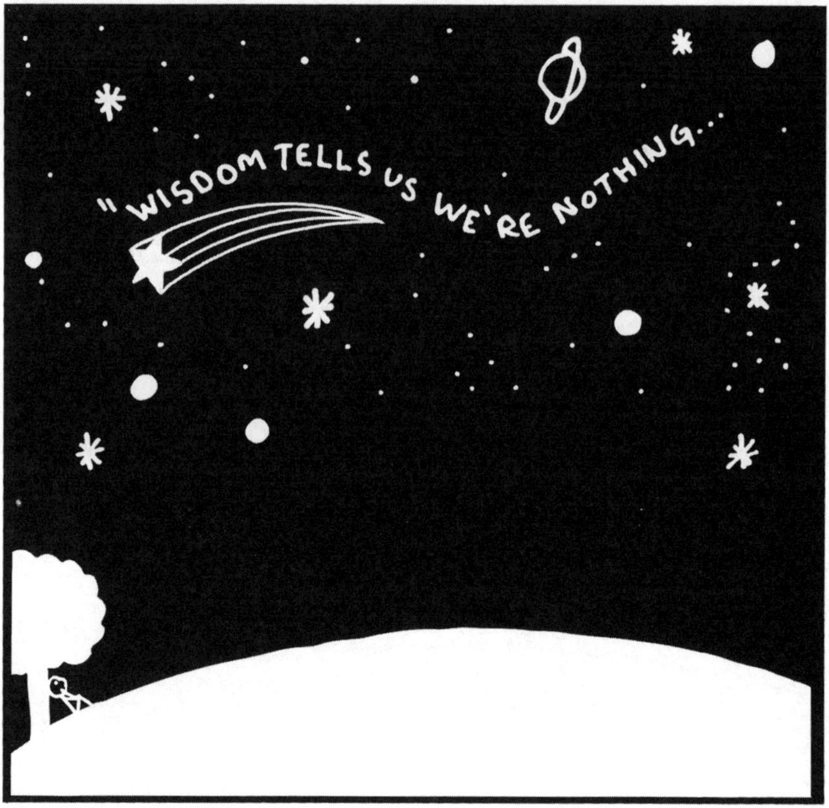
"WISDOM TELLS US WE'RE NOTHING...

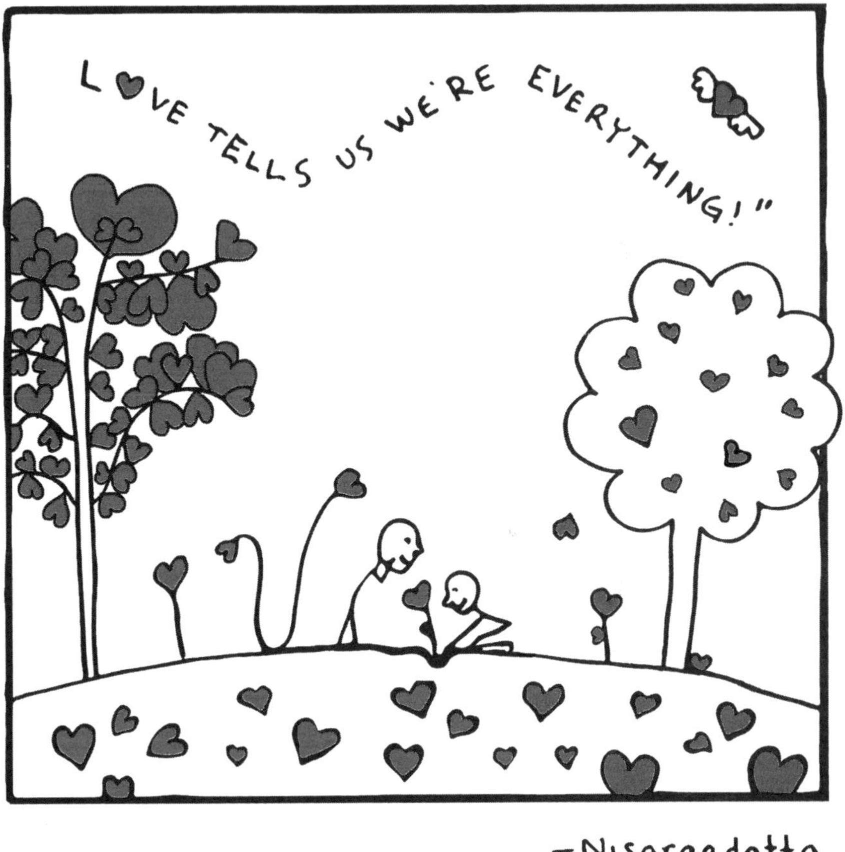
LOVE TELLS US WE'RE EVERYTHING!"

—Nisargadatta

Epilogue:

The Send-Off

The Send-Off

One of my favorite
Nice things to do
Is to let someone know
"I'm thinking of you."

On the last several pages
I drew just a few
Notes you can share
With your people too.

Whenever you want
To write to a friend
Just cut one out, fold it,
Sign it, and send!

Cut here

dharmacomics

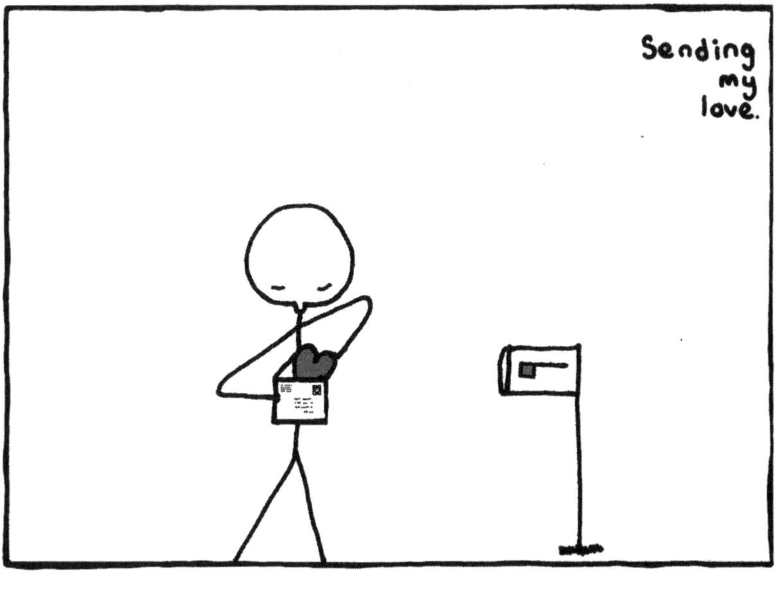
Sending
my
love.

My thoughts are with you...

...and I like them there.

dharmacomics

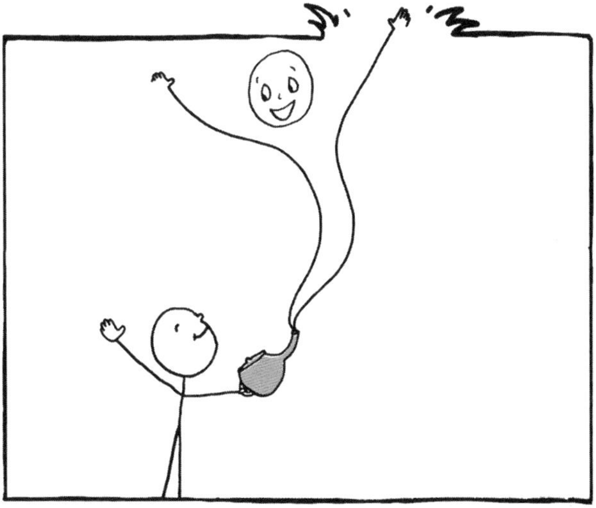

Thank you for believing in me!

dharmacomics

HAPPY BIRTHDAY!
from
afar

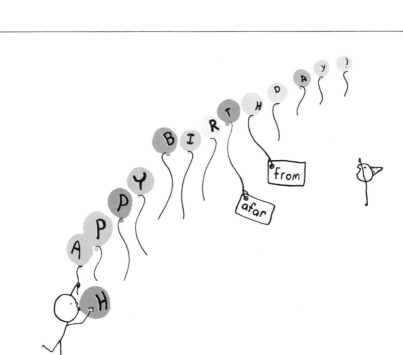

dharmacomics

This is for you. It's not perfect...

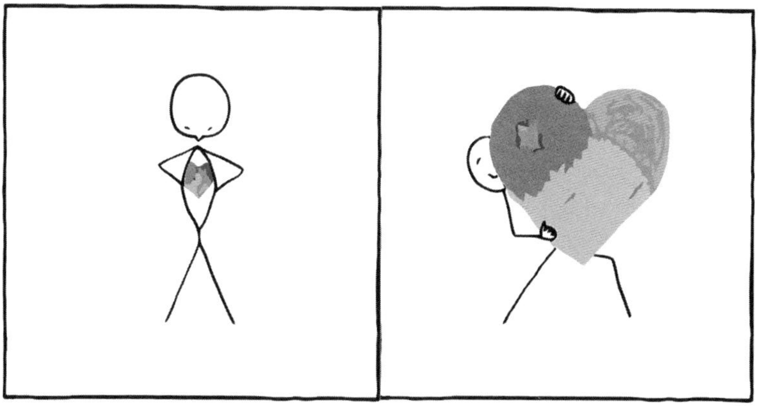

...but it's all i have. I hope you like it.

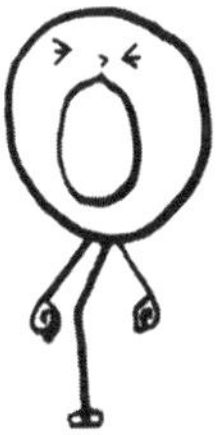

THE END

Nooooooo! Already!?
Could this be the end?
Isn't there some rule
we could bend?

YES. We discussed it
We all have agreed
We're simply not ready
To just see you leave.

So we made up a plan,
Oh please take a look!
We have decided:

TO STAY IN THIS BOOK!

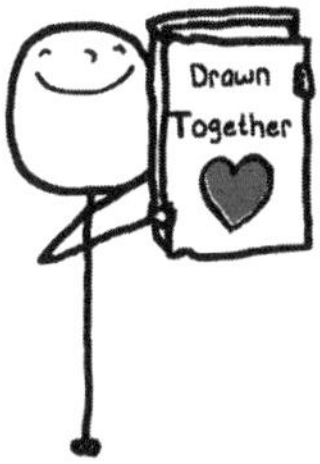
Drawn
Together

This way...

...You can come back here!
Whenever you need
Someone to love you
(Or something to read).

However you're feeling,
Happy or blue,
We promise to be here
Waiting for you.

Acknowledgments

Thank you to Erica Schreiber, Mat Vogels and Light-Lab Studios, the wonderful friends and geniuses who brought DharmaComics.com to life.

Thank you to Sasha Raskin, my agent at United Talent Agency, for reaching out to me that day. And thank you to my editor, Stephanie Bowen, at TarcherPerigee, for saying "Yes!" and then pushing me in the kindest possible way beyond what I thought I could do. Thank you to Will Dawes and Julie Lundy for your design support. Will KZ, "thank you" can't begin to cover it. I don't know if anything ever could.

Thank you to Joanna Phoenix, who brainstormed, edited, encouraged, and empathized every moment of this book journey with me. And to Scott Phoenix, for always reminding me to be proud, as well as teaching me the *most* necessary hot keys. Thank you to Sue Heilbronner, who always sees where I'm going long before I get there, and supports me every step of the way. And to my mom, who has loved me about as thoroughly as any parent ever could, and who now inspires me in the way she moves through the world in wonder.

To Diana Chapman, Jim Dethmer, and the rest of the Conscious Leadership Group: Thank you for helping me to find the "me" I had misplaced, and for all the fun we've had along the way. Thank you to the ServiceSpace family for teaching me everything I know about kindness, generosity, and humility. Thank you to Vlada and Michal Bortnik, who have been deep on this inner journey with me since it began. Thank you to Monte Nido for saving my life, and to Jonathan Foxx for helping to shape it.

Thank you to Om Skillet and the Shady Waffle gang who danced alongside me when Dharma Comics was born. Akhil Wable, thank you for that notebook you gave me in which I drew my first comic.

Thank you Tesa Silvestre, Joshua Home Edwards, Soren Gordhammer, Jack Kornfeld, and Dan Emmons for always reminding me where to look, and Keah Kalantari for always reminding me whom to trust.

A big thanks to the Pearlman family for your constant love and goofiness, and to the Heine side for your ever-present loyalty and love. Also to my second family in Colorado, who always call me back home to myself. And to Emily Crespin, for doing everything you did to get things going.

Shout-outs to Nathanael Wolfe and Logan Johnston, whose depth of care and quality of character are responsible for so much of the material here.

Thank you to my teachers: Rumi, Byron Katie, the Buddha, the Yoga, and the Dance, for lighting the North Star. Facebook, none of this would have been possible without you; I don't know if I will ever feel more grateful for any other experience. To Mokka, Arbor, Farley's in Oakland, and the Weathervane Cafe in Denver for keeping me company while I work. Thank you to Staedtler and Pigma markers and Borden & Riley paper. Thank you to pencils, erasers, and rulers. And, to whoever carved the first stick figure on a cave wall somewhere—you're a genius.

© MJ Mair-Reynaud 2016

About the Author

LEAH PEARLMAN is the creator and founder of Dharma Comics, a popular web comic series with a rapidly growing online audience of more than fifty thousand followers. She started her career as a technologist, working for Microsoft and then Facebook, where she cocreated both Facebook Pages and the Like button, the very features that later helped her comics spread. In 2010 she left Facebook to dedicate herself fully to a path of self-awareness and discovery, and continued drawing on life.

Dharma Comics have been featured in print magazines and newspapers such as *Inquiring Mind* and *Positive News*, online publications like KarmaTube and DailyGood, and books, including Dan Siegel's *New York Times* bestseller *Brainstorm*, and Jim Dethmer, Diana Chapman, and Kaley Warner Klemp's *The 15 Commitments of Conscious Leadership*. Leah has been interviewed on Eckhart Tolle's website TransformativeChange.org, and others, and has spoken at numerous conferences, including the immensely popular Wisdom 2.0. She currently lives in Berkeley, California, with two of her best friends, Scott and Joanna, who affectionately call her Animal. In addition to illustrating for herself and others she is often coaching, mentoring, investing, volunteering, traveling, and endlessly learning.

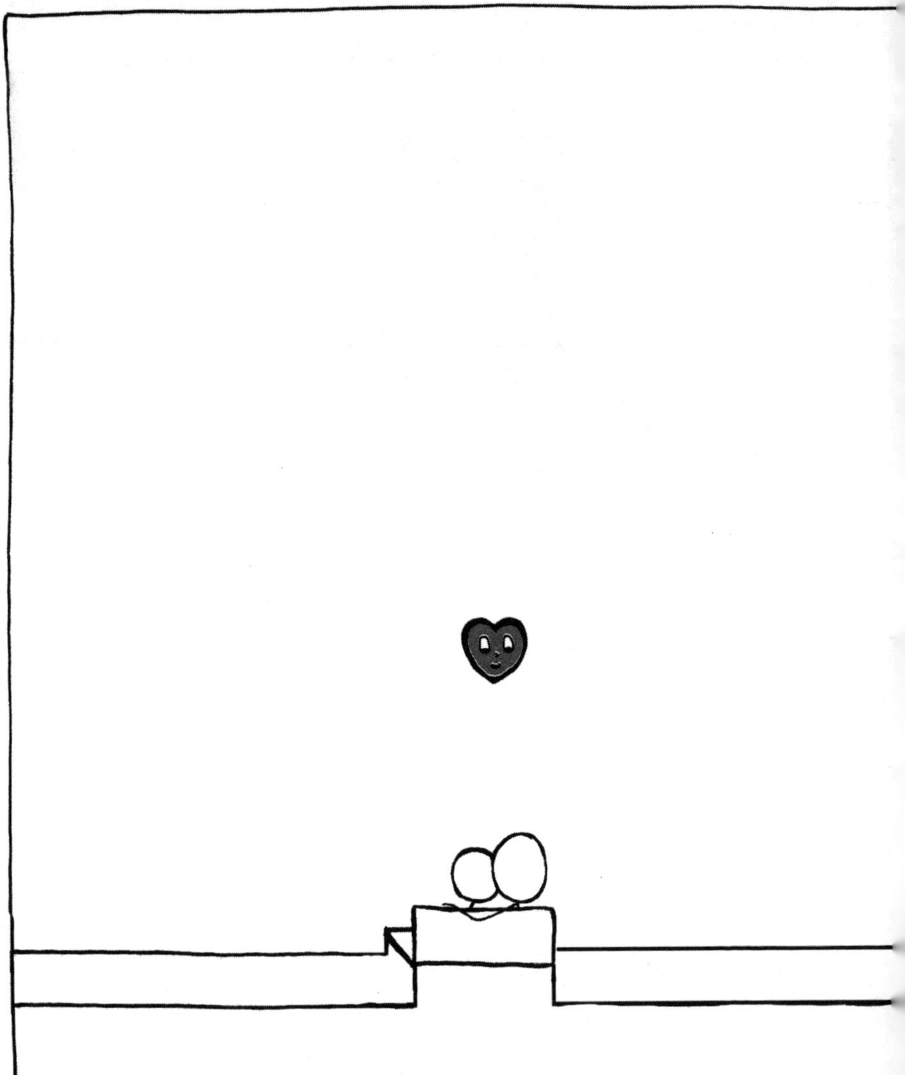
dharmacomics

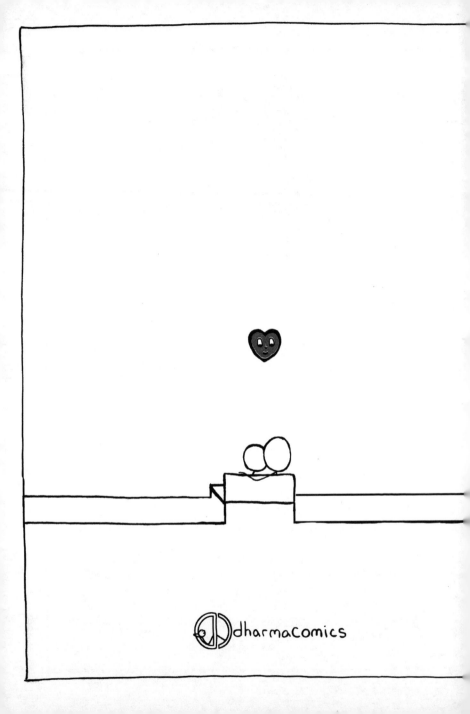